At Issue

Guns and Crime

Other Books in the At Issue Series:

At Issue

Guns and Crime

Louise Gerdes, Book Editor

GREENHAVEN PRESS

A part of Gale, Cengage Learning

GALE
CENGAGE Learning

Detroit • New York • San Francisco • New Haven, Conn • Waterville, Maine • London

Christine Nasso, *Publisher*
Elizabeth Des Chenes, *Managing Editor*

© 2008 Greenhaven Press, a part of Gale, Cengage Learning.

Gale and Greenhaven Press are registered trademarks used herein under license.

For more information, contact:
Greenhaven Press
27500 Drake Rd.
Farmington Hills, MI 48331-3535
Or you can visit our Internet site at gale.cengage.com

For product information and technology assistance, contact us at

Gale Customer Support, 1-800-877-4253
For permission to use material from this text or product, submit all requests online at
www.cengage.com/permissions

Further permissions questions can be emailed to permissionrequest@cengage.com

Articles in Greenhaven Press anthologies are often edited for length to meet page requirements. In addition, original titles of these works are changed to clearly present the main thesis and to explicitly indicate the author's opinion. Every effort is made to ensure that Greenhaven Press accurately reflects the original intent of the authors. Every effort has been made to trace the owners of copyrighted material.

Cover photograph reproduced by permission of Illustration Works.

LIBRARY OF CONGRESS CATALOGING-IN-PUBLICATION DATA

Guns and crime / Louise Gerdes, book editor.
   p. cm. -- (At issue)
   Includes bibliographical references and index.
   ISBN 978-0-7377-3918-3 (hardcover)
   ISBN 978-0-7377-3919-0 (pbk.)
   1. Gun control--United States. 2. Firearms and crime--United States. I. Gerdes, Louise I., 1953-
   HV7436.G87735 2008
   363.330973--dc22

                                                          2008012893

Printed in the United States of America
1 2 3 4 5 6 7 12 11 10 09 08

Contents

Introduction

Almost as soon as the media broadcast news of the tragic shooting at the Virginia Polytechnic Institute and State University, known as Virginia Tech, on April 16, 2007, commentators began to debate what could have prevented the deaths of thirty-two students and teachers at the hand of a gunman who took his own life at the Blacksburg, Virginia, school. Many commentators claim that college campuses are relatively safe places. "College students are almost 20 percent less likely than non-students of the same age to experience violence, and 93 percent of the violence against students occurs off campus," writes Paul Helmke of the Brady Campaign to Prevent Gun Violence. Nevertheless, the Virginia Tech massacre stepped up efforts at many campuses to make students even safer. One measure that some believe will improve campus safety is to improve campus communications systems. At Johns Hopkins University in Baltimore, for example, surveillance cameras are linked to computers that can alert campus and local police of suspicious activities. The University of Minnesota has installed electronic devices that can selectively lock and unlock doors and send emergency e-mail and phone messages.

Another strategy that some analysts think will increase campus safety is to better identify and provide treatment for students who pose a risk of dangerous or violent behavior. According to Russ Federman, director of counseling and psychological services at the University of Virginia, about 9 percent of the university's students sought psychological help in 2006. An American College Health Association (ACHA) survey, however, revealed that the stress of college might be more widespread. Nearly half of students surveyed by the ACHA reported feeling so depressed that they had difficulty functioning. Of these, nine out of one hundred had considered suicide. While most students with psychological problems pose no special risk, colleges "need to be able to communicate with one another, and sometimes with parents, when student threat of harm reaches a threshold where the University community is no longer safe," Federman claims.

Federal laws protecting privacy and patient confidentiality, however, make it difficult for mental health professionals and institutions to share information about students with mental health problems. In December 2005, a Virginia judge ordered Seung-Hui Cho, the Virginia Tech shooter, to receive outpatient psychiatric treatment, having found Cho to be "an imminent danger to himself." Questions remain, however, whether the university or Cho's parents knew of the adjudication. The Family and Education Rights and Privacy Act prevents universities from disclosing student records to anyone—even the students' parents. The Health Insurance Portability and Accountability Act prevents a health-care facility from communicating with an educational institution about any treatment it may have provided a student. Both Irwin Redlener, director of the National Center for Disaster Preparedness at Columbia University's School of Public Health and David Ward, president of the American Council on Education, have outlined steps for the federal government to help institutions better communicate about students who are potential threats. "I think we got a positive response from Congress . . . on putting some flexibility into the [privacy] law," claims Ward.

One of the most controversial recommendations to improve student safety is to allow guns on college campuses. Gun advocates claim that the Virginia Tech shooting is evidence that gun control is dangerous. They argue that those with concealed-carry gun permits might have reduced the death toll. The key to reducing gun violence on college campuses, gun advocates argue, is to increase penalties against criminals who use guns, not restrict the constitutional right of Americans to use firearms in self-defense. "The [Virginia Tech] shooting demands an immediate end to the gun-free-zone law, which leaves the nation's schools at the mercy of madmen," asserts Larry Pratt, Gun Owners of America executive director. "The solution," claims Pratt, "is to empower the most responsible people in America to be intermixed with potential victims so that they might have the opportunity to be the first responder to head off attacks such as the one at Virginia Tech." In fact, he maintains, the people who carry concealed firearms "are the folks who commit the fewest crimes in our society." If colleges allowed those with the right to carry concealed weapons to do so, students would be safer, gun advocates conclude. "Armed self-defense works," Pratt reasons; "disarmament kills."

Gun control proponents argue, on the other hand, that having guns on campuses only makes it easier for people like the Virginia Tech shooter. According to Paul Helmke of the Brady Campaign to Prevent Gun Violence, "Schools should be sanctuaries where students can grow and learn in an environment free from the risks of gunfire." The fact that shooters such as Cho invade colleges "is a reason to strengthen state and federal laws designed to keep guns away from people like the shooter at Virginia Tech, not to weaken policies that tightly restrict firearms on campus." Helmke also disputes the claim that gun owners are responsible people. He cites studies that reveal college gun owners to be more likely than the average student to use drugs such as cocaine or crack, vandalize property, engage in binge drinking, be arrested for driving under the influence of alcohol, be injured in an alcohol-related fight, and get in trouble with the police. "Binge-drinking, drug-using students are dangerous enough," Helmke maintains; "let's not give them guns."

Debates over what policies will best prevent horrific tragedies such as the mass murder at Virginia Tech remain hotly contested. Indeed, gun control remains one of the most hotly contested issues in the United States, a nation with not only one of the highest rates of civilian gun ownership but also one of the highest rates of gun-related injuries and deaths among the world's industrialized nations. The authors of the viewpoints in *At Issue: Guns and Crime* explore these and other issues concerning the nature and scope of the problem of guns and crime and the best policies to address it.

1

An Overview of Guns and Crime

Kenneth Jost

Kenneth Jost, who has been reporting on legal affairs since 1970, is the author of Supreme Court Yearbook *and a staff writer for* CQ Researcher.

Policy makers renewed the debate over what strategies best prevent or reduce gun violence following the April 16, 2007, shooting rampage at Virginia Tech, during which student Seung-hui Cho killed thirty-two people and himself. Some claim strengthening the background-check system will reduce gun violence, in part by disqualifying those with a history of mental illness. Mental health advocates argue, however, that targeting the mentally ill is unfair and will further stigmatize such groups. Still others argue for stricter gun-control laws, while gun advocates argue that laws allowing people to carry weapons will in fact deter crime and allow potential victims to defend themselves.

Seung-Hui Cho was a faceless e-mail address when he ordered a .22-caliber Walther P-22 pistol for $267 from Wisconsin gun dealer Eric Thompson via the Internet on Feb. 2, [2007]. The Virginia Tech senior drew no special attention when he picked the weapon up a week later from JND Pawnbrokers, near the spacious Blacksburg campus in southwest Virginia.

Cho was hardly more memorable a month later when he traveled in person to Roanoke Firearms about 35 miles away and made a $571 credit-card purchase of a 9 mm Glock 19 pistol and 50 rounds of ammunition. "A clean-cut college kid," said John Markell, the store's owner, quoting the after-the-fact description from the clerk who handled the March 13 transaction.

Twice, the Korean-born Cho presented the necessary identification—his Virginia driver's license, checkbook and immigration card—to complete the federal background check required for handgun purchasers. Twice, computers took only moments to display the needed authorization: *proceed.*

Nothing particularly distinguished Cho's transactions from any of the other estimated 2 million handgun purchases in the United States each year. Thompson in Wisconsin and the gun dealers in Virginia had no reason to know or even suspect that Cho was an extremely troubled young man whose bizarre and sometimes aggressive behavior had disturbed his parents, schoolmates and teachers for years.

Two years earlier, in fact, a state judge in Virginia had ordered Cho to receive outpatient psychiatric treatment after finding him to be "an imminent danger to himself" because of mental illness. Had they known that history, people at both stores said afterward, they would not have sold Cho the guns.

The [gun] debate remains volatile in a country with what experts say is probably the highest rate of civilian gun ownership in the world.

But they did. And so, on the morning of April 16 [2007] Cho used the weapons to kill 32 people on the Virginia Tech campus before taking his own life with a final shot to the head. The death toll—along with the 29 others wounded—marked Cho's intricately plotted, alienation-driven rampage as the worst mass school shooting in U.S. history.

Renewing the Gun Debate

The massacre left the 26,000-student state university in a state of shock and brought forth outpourings of sympathy from officials and private citizens around the world. Hardly any time had passed, however, before the tragedy renewed the perennial debate in the United States over the rules for buying, selling and possessing firearms and the penalties for misusing them.

The debate remains volatile in a country with what experts say is probably the highest rate of civilian gun ownership in the world and also the highest rate of gun-related injuries and deaths among major industrialized nations. Americans own what has been variously estimated as 200 million to 250 million firearms, around one-third of them handguns. Surveys indicate that more than 40 percent of all U.S. households own at least one firearm.

Meanwhile, the number of gun-related deaths in the United States has been around 30,000 per year for more than two decades, according to the federal Centers for Disease Control and Prevention. For 2004—the most recent year available—the number included 11,624 homicides and 16,750 suicides.

> *[Gun control advocates] call for strengthening enforcement of existing federal laws barring possession of firearms.*

Gun advocates—including the powerful, 3-million-member National Rifle Association (NRA)—defend what they view as an individual constitutional right to use firearms in hunting, sport shooting and self-defense. They argue that gun owners and dealers are already subject to a web of federal, state and local firearm laws and regulations. The key to reducing gun violence, they say, lies with tougher penalties against criminals who use guns, instead of more restrictions on gun owners.

"We have adequate gun laws on the books," says Andrew Arulanandam, the NRA's director of public affairs. "If a crime occurs, those criminals need to be prosecuted to the fullest extent of the law. The question becomes how do you make something that is already illegal more illegal."

Gun control advocates, including the influential Brady Campaign to Prevent Gun Violence, counter by depicting the widespread availability of handguns as a primary factor in the high rate of gun-related injuries and deaths. They call for strengthening enforcement of existing federal laws barring possession of firearms by certain criminals, drug users and people with mental illness. They also favor restrictions on certain specific types of weapons or ammunition and generally oppose laws favored by gun groups easing the roles for the carrying of concealed weapons.

"We have weak, almost nonexistent gun laws in this country," says Paul Helmke, president of the Brady Campaign and its affiliated education arm, the Brady Center to Prevent Gun Violence. "And we're seeing almost the natural result of having weak, nonexistent gun laws with the Virginia Tech shootings and the 32 murders that happen every day [in the United States]."

Advocating Familiar Arguments

The post Virginia Tech debate features familiar arguments over the effectiveness of the landmark Gun Control Act of 1968 and the National Instant Criminal Background Check System, established in 1998 to enable gun dealers to enforce the act's prohibitions on gun ownership by criminals and others. But Cho's history of mental illness highlights an issue given less attention in the past: the conflicting federal and state definitions used to disqualify people with a history of mental illness from owning a gun.

Mental health groups, however, caution against viewing mental illness as an indicator of potential violence. "It's very easy and very tempting when something as horrible as Virginia Tech occurs to assume that mental illness correlates with a propensity for violence," says Ron Honberg, director of policy and legal affairs for the National Alliance on Mental Illness. "That's not borne out for the majority of people with mental illness."

The Blacksburg massacre is also giving new and urgent attention to questions of safety and security on the nation's college campuses. Some gun advocacy groups see Cho's ability to carry out the shootings, including the nine-minute rampage inside a classroom building, as an argument for lifting the ban on guns imposed by most schools, including Virginia Tech.

"The latest school shooting demands an immediate end to the gun-free-zone law, which leaves the nation's schools at the mercy of madmen," said [Larry] Pratt, executive director of Gun Owners of America, in a statement released on the day of the massacre. "It is irresponsibly dangerous to tell citizens that they may not have guns at schools."

Campus law enforcement officials, along with other police groups as well as gun control supporters, disagree. "The only folks who should have firearms on a campus are those people who are sworn and authorized to protect and are duly trained to do that," says Steven Healy, director of public safety at Princeton University and president of the International Association of Campus Law Enforcement Administrators.

Legislative and Judicial Debates

Congress is considering legislation previously introduced to give states financial incentives to improve their reporting to the background-check system in hopes of plugging gaps in enforcement of the federal restrictions on gun possession. But the political climate is widely viewed as unfavorable for any broader measures. "In the very short run, I don't expect we'll do anything seriously," says David Hemenway, a professor at the Harvard School of Public Health and longtime gun control advocate.

Meanwhile, gun advocacy groups are hoping to preserve a major victory in the courts: a federal appeals court on March 9 [2007] struck down Washington's strict local law banning possession of handguns even in private homes. In a 2-1 decision, the U.S. Court of Appeals for the District of Columbia Circuit ruled that the 1976 measure violates the Second Amendment's guarantee of a right to bear arms.

The ruling contradicts the view long held but recently being reconsidered that the Bill of Rights provision protects state militias but does not establish an individual's right to own firearms. Washington Mayor Adrian Fenty is weighing whether to try rewriting the ordinance or to ask the Supreme Court to review the decision.

With the Virginia Tech shootings still very much a scar on the national psyche, [several] major gun policy questions [are] being considered. . . .

Mental Illness and Background Checks

In December 2005, midway through his sophomore year, Seung-Hui Cho was referred to a mental health clinic by Virginia Tech police after he had threatened suicide following two female students' complaints he was harassing them. In a hearing held Dec. 14 [2005] after an overnight evaluation, special judge Paul Barnett found Cho to be "an imminent danger to himself" and ordered outpatient treatment.

The judicial finding arguably disqualified Cho from buying a handgun under federal law. Virginia authorities, however, never fed that information into the federal background-check system. Why not? Unlike the federal law, Virginia's corresponding law specifically requires commitment to a mental hospital to block an applicant from purchasing a firearm.

The information gap that might have blocked or at least delayed Cho from buying the guns he used in his rampage is not unique to Virginia. In fact, the pro–gun control group Third Way rates Virginia among the best in reporting mental health information to the FBI's instant-check system. Overall, the group reports, only 22 states provide mental health records to the system—"rendering this provision of the law useless in most states."

> *Legislation to improve the background-check system ... has the backing not only of gun control groups but also of the NRA.*

Legislation to improve the background-check system—reintroduced in Congress after Virginia Tech—has the backing not only of gun control groups but also of the NRA, the most powerful of the gun advocacy groups. "Someone who's dangerous to himself or others because of mental illness shouldn't get a gun," says the Brady Center's Helmke. "That's what the law says."

"We've been on record for decades that records of those adjudicated as mentally defective and deemed to be a danger to others or to themselves should be part of the national instant-check system and not be allowed to own a firearm," says NRA spokesman Arulanandam. "The mental health lobby and the medical lobby are the impediments—they are against release of the records."

The rival Gun Owners of America, however, opposes any strengthening of a background-check system that it calls both ineffective and intrusive. "All the background checks in the world will not stop bad guys from getting firearms," the group's Web site declares.

Singling Out the Mentally Ill

Mental health groups are raising more specific concerns about the legislation. They warn that more extensive reporting of people with a history of mental illness will expose them to discrimination and prejudice and possibly deter some people from seeking treatment altogether. "We have real grave concerns about people with mental illness being a population that's singled out," says Honberg, at the National Alliance on Mental Illness.

"Even if someone was severely disabled 30 years ago, we have plenty of examples of people who have gone on to recover and are living independently and are working and are upstanding citizens," Honberg adds. "Do we want to include all those people in the database?"

The Gun Control Act of 1968 prohibits possession of a firearm by anyone "adjudicated as a mental defective" or who has been committed to any mental institution. The law defines a "mental defective" as a person who "is a danger to himself or others" or "lacks the mental capacity to contract or manage his own affairs" as a result of "marked subnormal intelligence" or "mental illness." The regulations broadly define adjudication to include "a determination by a court, board, commission or other lawful authority."

The statutory phrase "mental defective" is both outmoded and stigmatizing, Honberg says. "It's a term no one has used for 30 to 40 years," he says. The regulatory provisions, he adds, are "vague and potentially overbroad."

The bills pending in Congress leave the definitions unchanged. Honberg suggests the mental health provisions should be amended to include "some durational limitation" as well as a process for someone to petition for removal from the list. More broadly, he worries about possible abuses from a more rigorously maintained list.

"We're concerned that the very agency charged with managing these records, the FBI, maintains a whole lot of other lists," Honberg says. "We're talking about a population that is oftentimes victimized by breaches of confidentiality and prejudice."

Gun Owners of America seconds those concerns. "What type of record are we talking about . . .?" asks Mike Hammond, a legal and legislative adviser to the group.

The Brady Center's Helmke counters that states are being asked only for court records. "It's not checking hospital records or doctors' records," he says. "This shouldn't be something that discourages people from getting help for problems."

In Virginia, meanwhile, Democratic Gov. Tim Kaine has moved to tighten the state's law on access to guns for people with histories of mental illness. On April 30 [2007], he ordered state agencies "to consider any involuntary treatment order . . . whether inpatient or outpatient" as disqualifying an applicant from buying a gun.

Carrying Concealed Weapons

When a disgruntled student at Appalachian School of Law in southwestern Virginia went on a deadly shooting rampage in January 2002, two students—one current and one former police officer—dashed to their cars to get their own guns. As gun advocates tell the story, former police officer Mikael Gross and sheriff's deputy Tracy Bridges brandished their weapons at the shooter, who dropped his gun and was then subdued with the help of two other, unarmed students.

No one confronted Cho, however, during the shootings in the West Ambler Johnston dormitory or the nine-minute rampage inside Norris Hall. One reason, gun advocates say, is Virginia Tech's ban on private possession of firearms on campus—a proscription Gross and Bridges apparently disregarded at the Appalachian law school.

"If there were more responsible, armed people on campuses, mass murder would be harder," writes Glenn Reynolds, a law professor at the University of Tennessee and author of the conservative blog InstaPundit.

Gun advocates point to the Appalachian law school incident as one among many examples showing "defensive gun use" is both more common and more effective in protecting lives and property than widely assumed or acknowledged by gun control supporters. They favor easing laws on carrying concealed weapons and repealing "gun-free zone" laws that prohibit carrying a weapon in specific places, such as campuses.

Police organizations and gun control advocates . . . depict defensive gun use as rare and risky.

Police organizations and gun control advocates disagree. They depict defensive gun use as rare and risky and widespread carrying of weapons as an invitation to more gun violence. And they specifically dispute any suggestion that an armed student or teacher might have been able to prevent or limit Cho's rampage at Virginia Tech.

"Every time I play that out, I come up with worse results," says Healy of the campus police group. "When you have untrained people with obviously someone who was extremely mentally ill and several [police] agencies responding simultaneously, it's a recipe for disaster."

"What we're wishing for is that [cowboy movie hero] John Wayne or James Bond had been sitting in the classroom," says the Brady Center's Helmke, who as mayor of Ft. Wayne, Ind., directed the city's police department before his present position. "In the real world, it doesn't work that way."

Using Guns in Self-Defense

The use of guns in self-defense has been an especially contentious piece of the gun policy debate since the early 1990s, when [Gary] Kleck [a professor at Florida State University's College of Criminology and Criminal Justice] produced research that is now used to estimate as many as 2.5 million defensive uses of guns per year in the United States. Seven years later, economist John Lott, then at the University of Chicago, coauthored a study claiming that states with laws making it easier to carry concealed handguns had lower overall crime rates than those without such laws.

Expanded later into books, both studies drew fire immediately from gun control organizations on policy grounds and from like-minded academics, who have exhaustively documented what they regard as patent flaws in the statistical methods used. Whatever the validity of the studies, they both became useful ammunition for gun advocates in resisting additional gun measures and, in particular, in easing laws allowing qualified citizens to carry concealed weapons.

With eased carry laws on the books today in 40 states, gun advocates continue to endorse them and urge the rest of the states to follow suit. "Law-abiding people have the right to defend themselves," says the NRA's Arulanandam. "The sad reality is that just because you're outside your home, you're not immune from crime. Crime can happen to anyone, anywhere."

Gun control supporters, on the other hand, oppose what they call the "radical liberalization" of concealed carry laws pushed by gun advocates. "An armed society is an at-risk society," a Brady Center position paper declares. The paper cautions that people "underestimate" the difficulty of successfully using a gun for self-defense and also warns that the availability of weapons allows minor arguments to escalate into "deadly gun play."

Lott, now a visiting professor at the State University of New York, Binghamton, and Kleck continue to defend their studies and their policy conclusion. Lott, for example, strongly argues against laws creating gun-free zones. "You unintentionally make it safer for the criminal because there's less for them to worry about," he says.

People using guns in self-defense rarely injure themselves and typically succeed in preventing injury or loss of property at the criminal's hands.

Kleck insists that despite contrary examples cited by gun control opponents, people using guns in self-defense rarely injure themselves and typically succeed in preventing injury or loss of property at the criminal's hands. Interestingly, Kleck rejects Lott's conclusion that concealed-carry laws lower overall crime rates and points to studies showing that only a small fraction of people ever actually carry weapons. But Kleck says he still favors those laws on self-defense grounds.

Harvard's Hemenway, however, insists that guns represent a greater risk than a potential benefit for public safety. "There's strong evidence that where there are more guns generally, there are lots, lots, lots more gun problems," he says.

As for guns on campus, Hemenway professes horror. "I would expect it would rarely do much good, and it has enormous potential for harm," he says. "The notion of allowing drunk frat boys to go around campus armed, that would be scary for me."

2

Gun Violence Is a Serious Problem

Juliet A. Leftwich

Juliet A. Leftwich is senior counsel of Legal Community Against Violence, a national law center formed in the wake of the 101 California Street assault-weapon massacre in San Francisco that killed eight people and the gunman on July 1, 1993.

On average, guns kill as many people each day as were killed in the April 16, 2007, Virginia Tech shooting that claimed thirty-two innocent lives and the life of the shooter. However, unlike high-profile school shootings, most of the thirty thousand gun deaths in the United States each year receive little media attention. Americans should be as outraged by the more than three thousand gun deaths every six weeks in the United States as they are by the similar number of American soldiers killed in Iraq in the first four years of the war. Americans should demand that the federal government enact gun laws that will reduce gun violence at home.

On March 13, 1996, a former scoutmaster named Thomas Hamilton used four legally purchased handguns to slaughter 16 children and a teacher at an elementary school in Dunblane, Scotland. In response to the shooting, Great Britain banned virtually all handguns.

The U.S. Response to Shooting Rampages

Three years later, on April 20, 1999, Columbine High School students Eric Harris and Dylan Klebold went on a shooting rampage in Colorado, killing 12 of their classmates and a teacher before ending their own lives. The federal government's response to the Columbine massacre? None, despite the fact that six other school shootings had taken place in America in the preceding 19 months.

Nearly eight years to the day after Columbine, on April 16, 2007, college student Seung-Hui Cho shot and killed 32 people at Virginia Tech before killing himself. That mass shooting—the worst in modern U.S. history—came only six months after five young girls were gunned down at an Amish schoolhouse in Pennsylvania. Was the federal government finally prompted to take action to prevent similar tragedies from happening in the future? Hardly.

In fact, the first statement from the White House after the Virginia Tech shooting was that President [George W.] Bush supported the "right to bear arms." Later, he expressed condolences to the grieving families, but said that "now's not the time" to discuss any specific federal response to the tragedy. This sentiment was echoed by several members of Congress, including leading Democrats.

Perhaps it should come as no surprise, then, that with the six-month anniversary of the Virginia Tech shootings approaching next week [October 2007], Congress still hasn't passed any new gun laws.

On average 32 people are killed in gun homicides each day in America—that's the equivalent of a daily Virginia Tech shooting.

How much more blood must be spilled before Congress decides that the time has come to take action? Guns are used to kill nearly 30,000 people each year in this country in homicides, suicides and unintentional shootings. Although most gun deaths receive little media attention, on average 32 people are killed in gun homicides each day in America—that's the equivalent of a daily Virginia Tech shooting.

Some states, impatient with the gun lobby's stranglehold over Congress, have taken action to fill the huge gaps in federal law. California, for example, has adopted laws to close the "private sale" loophole, which allows unlicensed persons to sell guns without conducting background checks on prospective purchasers. [California] also mandates the retention of handgun sales records, requires handgun safety certificates for handgun purchasers, bans assault weapons and "junk guns," requires a 10-day waiting period and limits gun sales to one per person per month.

In addition, the [2007 California] Legislature passed a groundbreaking "microstamping" bill which, if signed into law by Gov. Arnold Schwarzenegger, will allow law enforcement to trace cartridge cases found at crime scenes to the firearms that fired them. The governor has until Oct. 14 [2007] to sign the legislation, which is supported by more than 65 police chiefs and sheriffs and several major law enforcement organizations statewide. [Schwarzenegger signed the bill into law on October 13, 2007.]

Although strong state laws are important, they are not enough, standing alone, to keep Americans safe from gun violence. Given the ease with which guns cross state borders, what we need—and must demand—are comprehensive federal laws to regulate the manufacture, sale and possession of firearms.

A Need for Federal Laws

The United States has the weakest gun laws of all of the industrialized nations in the world (and, not surprisingly, the highest rate of firearm-related deaths). Congress could take many concrete steps short of a handgun ban to significantly reduce our nation's epidemic of gun violence.

First and foremost, Congress could close the private sale loophole and require background checks on all prospective gun purchasers. Under current federal law, only federally licensed firearms dealers are required to perform background checks. Private sales, however, account for approximately 40 percent of all gun sales. As a result, except in the handful of states (like California) that have moved to close this loophole, criminals, young people and the mentally ill are easily able to buy guns from private sellers at gun shows and other locations nationwide.

Congress could also require registration of guns and licensing of gun owners, similar to the way our laws require registration of cars and licensing of drivers. Currently, the federal government has no idea who owns firearms in this country (indeed, thanks to the NRA [National Rifle Association] federal law actually prohibits the use of background check records to create any system of registration of firearms or firearms owners).

Registration laws are critical, however, because they allow law enforcement to quickly trace crime guns back to the individuals who purchased them, and to return lost or stolen firearms to their lawful owners. When registration laws require annual renewal and additional background checks, they also help ensure that gun owners remain eligible to possess firearms and do not illegally transfer their guns to others. Strong licensing laws are essential because they require gun owners to demonstrate their familiarity with existing gun laws and their ability to handle and store firearms safely. Registration and licensing laws are the cornerstone of responsible gun policy in industrialized nations worldwide.

In addition, Congress could provide financial incentives to the states to submit all of their criminal and mental health records to the National Instant Criminal Background Check System (NICS). Currently, many prohibited persons are able to pass background checks because state records—including more than 90 percent of disqualifying mental health records and 25 percent of criminal convictions—have not been entered in NICS. (The House passed a long-languishing bill to provide such financial incentives [in spring 2007], but only after the NRA added last-minute amendments to compromise the legislation. That bill has stalled in the Senate.)

Moreover, Congress could:

Authorize the Consumer Product Safety Commission to regulate firearms (the Consumer Product Safety Act currently exempts firearms and ammunition—and tobacco—from its requirements).

Adopt a waiting period to give law enforcement adequate time to conduct background checks and allow gun purchasers an opportunity to "cool off."

Limit the number of guns an individual may purchase at any one time (to prevent gun traffickers from buying large quantities of firearms and reselling them on the black market).

Finally, Congress could undo the significant damage inflicted during the Bush administration by reinstating, and then strengthening, the assault weapon ban (which was allowed to expire in 2004 despite overwhelming public and law enforcement support), repealing the law granting the gun industry unprecedented immunity from most civil lawsuits (introduced by former NRA board member Sen. Larry Craig), repealing the so-called Tiahrt Amendment, which prohibits the Bureau of Alcohol, Tobacco, Firearms and Explosives from disclosing crime gun trace data (used to identify patterns of gun trafficking and released to the public until 2004), and repealing the law requiring firearm purchaser records to be destroyed after 24 hours.

The Second Amendment

Contrary to the gun lobby's mantra about the "right to bear arms," the Second Amendment provides no obstacle to such laws. Nearly seventy years ago, in *U.S. v. Miller*, 307 U.S. 174

(1939), the Supreme Court held that the "obvious purpose" of the Second Amendment was to "assure the continuation and render possible the effectiveness" of the state militia. Since *Miller*, lower courts have rejected more than 200 Second Amendment challenges to firearm-related laws. Only one federal appellate decision in American history has struck down a gun law on Second Amendment grounds: *Parker v. District of Columbia*, 478 F.3d 370 (D.C. Cir. 2007), which involved a challenge to the District's laws banning most handgun possession.

That case, decided in March 2007, held that the Second Amendment guarantees an individual right to possess firearms unrelated to service in a well-regulated militia. The District is seeking U.S. Supreme Court review of the decision (now entitled *District of Columbia v. Heller*). If review is granted, and if the court follows its own precedent, the lower court decision should be reversed. [The Court agreed to review the case in November 2007; arguments began in March 2008.]

Guns claim the lives of more than 3,000 people [in the United States] every six weeks. Where's the outrage about that?

When high-profile shootings like Columbine and Virginia Tech rock our nation, most Americans react with shock, horror and anguish. For some reason, however, those emotions have not yet translated into demands that our federal government actually do something to stop the carnage, despite the fact that opinion polls consistently show public support for stronger gun laws. Americans are outraged by the Iraq War and have begun to demand that the U.S. change its war policy. That outrage is completely justified: The Iraq War has taken the lives of more than 3,000 American soldiers.

But guns claim the lives of more than 3,000 people here at home every six weeks. Where's the outrage about that? The bloodbath at home will continue, day after day, year after year, unless and until the public demands that our federal legislators enact the common sense gun laws that we need.

3

The Media Overlook the Role of Guns in Preventing Crime

John R. Lott Jr.

John R. Lott Jr., an economist, is at present a visiting research scientist at the University of Maryland. He is the author of The Bias Against Guns.

People use guns to prevent crimes more often than they use guns to commit crimes. Unfortunately, media silence on the defensive use of guns prevents people from learning that guns are an effective way to confront violence. In fact, 95 percent of the time, simply brandishing a gun will thwart a crime. In January 2002 at Appalachian School of Law, for example, two students with guns confronted a shooter and put an end to his shooting rampage. Guns clearly help people defend themselves in the face of a threat when few alternatives are available.

I often give talks to audiences explaining that research by me and others shows that guns are used much more often to fend off crimes than to commit them. People are very surprised to learn that survey data show that guns are used defensively by private citizens in the U.S. anywhere from 1.5 to 3.4 million times a year. A question I hear repeatedly is: "If defensive gun use occurs so often, why haven't I ever heard of even one story?"

The Defensive Use of Guns

Obviously anecdotal stories published in newspapers can't prove how numerous these events are, but they can at least deal with the question of whether these events even occur.

John R. Lott Jr., "Half Cocked: Why Most of What You See in the Media About Guns Is Wrong," *American Enterprise*, July 1, 2003. Reproduced by permission of the author.

During 2001, I did two detailed searches on defensive gun uses: one for the period covering March 11 to 17 of that year, and another for the period July 22 to 28. While these searches were not meant to be comprehensive, I found a total of 40 defensive gun uses over those two weeks. . . .

Life and death stories represent only a tiny fraction of defensive gun uses. A survey of 1,015 people I conducted during November and December 2002 indicates that 2.3 million defensive gun uses occurred nationwide in 2001. Guns do make it easier to commit bad deeds, but they also make it easier for people to defend themselves where few alternatives are available. That is why it is so important that people receive an accurate, balanced accounting of how guns are used. Unfortunately, the media are doing a very poor job of that today.

Though . . . simply brandishing a gun stops crimes 95 percent of the time, it is very rare to see a story of such an event reported in the media.

Though my survey indicates that simply brandishing a gun stops crimes 95 percent of the time, it is very rare to see a story of such an event reported in the media. A dead gunshot victim on the ground is highly newsworthy, while a criminal fleeing after a woman points a gun is apparently not considered news at all. That's not impossible to understand; after all, no shots were fired, no crime was committed, and no one is even sure what crime would have been committed had a weapon not been drawn.

In other words, airplane crashes get news coverage, while successful take-offs and landings do not. Even though fewer than one out of 1,000 defensive gun uses result in the death of the attacker, the newsman's penchant for drama means that the bloodier cases are usually covered. Even in the rare cases where guns are used to shoot someone, injuries are about six times more frequent than deaths. You wouldn't know this from the stories the media choose to report.

Stopping a Shooting Spree

But much more than a bias toward bad news and drama goes into the media's selective reporting on gun usage. Why, for instance, does the torrential coverage of public shooting sprees fail to acknowledge when such attacks are aborted by citizens with guns? In January 2002, a shooting left three dead at the Appalachian Law School in Virginia. The event made international headlines and produced more calls for gun control.

Yet one critical fact was missing from virtually all the news coverage: The attack was stopped by two students who had guns in their cars.

The fast responses of Mikael Gross and Tracy Bridges undoubtedly saved many lives. Mikael was outside the law school returning from lunch when Peter Odighizuwa started shooting. Tracy was in a classroom waiting for class to start. When the shots rang out, chaos erupted. Mikael and Tracy were prepared to do something more constructive: Both immediately ran to their cars and got their guns, then approached the shooter from different sides. Thus confronted, the attacker threw his gun down.

Isn't it remarkable that out of 208 news stories (from a Nexis-Lexis search) in the week after the event, just four mentioned that the students who stopped the shooter had guns? A typical description of the event in the *Washington Post*: "Three students pounced on the gunman and held him until help arrived." New York's *Newsday* noted only that the attacker was "restrained by students." Many stories mentioned the law-enforcement or military backgrounds of these student heroes, but virtually all of the media, in discussing how the killer was stopped, said things such as: "students tackled the man while he was still armed" "students tackled the gunman" the attacker "dropped his gun after being confronted by students, who then tackled him to the ground" or "students ended the rampage by confronting and then tackling the gunman, who dropped his weapon."

In all, 72 stories described how the attacker was stopped, without mentioning that the heroes had guns. Yet 68 stories provided precise details on the gun used by the attacker: The *New York Times* made sure to point out it was "a .380 semiautomatic handgun"; the *Los Angeles Times* noted it was "a .380-caliber semiautomatic pistol."

A week and a half after the assault, I appeared on a radio program in Los Angeles along with Tracy Bridges, one of the Appalachian Law School heroes. Tracy related how "shocked" he had been by the news coverage. Though he had carefully described to over 50 reporters what had happened, explaining how he had to point his gun at the attacker and yell at him to drop his gun, the media had consistently reported that the incident had ended by the students "tackling" the killer. When I relayed what the *Washington Post* had reported, Tracy quickly mentioned that he had spent a considerable amount of time talking face-to-face with reporter Maria Glod of the *Post*. He seemed stunned that this conversation had not resulted in a more accurate rendition of what had occurred. . . .

It's no wonder people find it hard to believe that guns are used in self-defense 2 million times a year: Reporting on these events is systematically suppressed.

The Danger of Media Bias

Selective reporting of crimes such as the Appalachian Law School incident isn't just poor journalism; it could actually endanger people's lives. By turning a case of defensive gun use into a situation where students merely "overpowered a gunman" the media give potential victims the wrong impression of what works when confronted with violence. Research consistently shows that having a gun (usually just showing it) is the safest way to respond to any type of criminal assault.

It's no wonder people find it hard to believe that guns are used in self-defense 2 million times a year: Reporting on these events is systematically suppressed. When was the last time you saw a story in the national news about a private citizen using his gun to stop a crime? Media decisions to cover only the crimes committed with guns—and not the crimes stopped with them—have a real impact on people's perceptions of the desirability of guns. . . .

Moreover, the few defensive news stories that got coverage were almost all local stories. Though articles about gun crimes are treated as both local and national stories, defensive uses of guns are given only local coverage in the rare instances they run at all. In the full sample of defensive gun-use stories I have collected, less than 1 percent ran outside the local coverage area. News about guns only seems to travel if it's bad.

This helps explain why residents of urban areas are so in favor of gun control. Most crime occurs in the biggest cities, and urbanites are bombarded with tales of gun-facilitated crime. It happens that most defensive gun uses also occur in these same big cities, but they simply aren't reported.

This imbalance isn't just limited to newspapers. Take the 1999 special issue of *Newsweek* entitled "America Under the Gun." Though over 15,000 words and numerous graphics were provided on the topic of gun ownership, there was not one mention of self-defense with a firearm. Under the heading "America's Weapons of Choice," the table captions were: "Top firearms traced to crimes, 1998"; "Firearm deaths per 100,000 people"; and "Percent of homicides using firearms." Nothing at all on "Top firearms used in self-defense," or "Rapes, homicides, and other crimes averted with firearms." The magazine's graphic, gut-wrenching pictures all showed people who had been wounded by guns. No images were offered of people who had used guns to save lives or prevent injuries.

To investigate television coverage, I collected stories reported during 2001 on the evening news broadcasts and morning news shows of ABC, CBS, and NBC. Several segments focused on the increase in gun sales after [the terrorist attacks of] September 11, 2001, and a few of these shows actually went so far as to list the desire for self-defense as a reason for that increase. But despite slightly over 190,000 words of coverage on gun crimes, merely 580 words, on a single news broadcast, were devoted to the use of a gun to block crime—a story about an off-duty police officer who helped stop a school shooting. Not one of the networks mentioned any other defensive gun use—certainly not one carried out by a civilian.

The Experts Cited

Another place where the predilections of reporters color the news about guns is in the choice of authorities quoted. An analysis of *New York Times* news articles over the last two years [2001–2003] reveals that *Times* reporters overwhelmingly cite pro-gun-control academics in their articles. From February 2000 to February 2002, the *Times* cited nine strongly pro-control academics a total of 20 times; one neutral academic once; and no academic who was skeptical that gun control reduces crime. Not once. The same pro-control academics were referenced again and again: Philip Cook of Duke, Alfred Blumstein at Carnegie Mellon, Garen Wintemute of the University of California at Davis.

This imbalance in experts interviewed cannot be explained away by an inability to find academics who are dubious about most gun control laws. Two hundred ninety-four academics from institutions as diverse as Harvard, Stanford, Northwestern, the University of Pennsylvania, and UCLA [University of California at Los Angeles] released an open letter to Congress in 1999 stating that the new gun laws being proposed at that time were "ill advised." These professors were economists, lawyers, and criminologists. None of these academics was quoted in *New York Times* reports on guns over a two-year period. . . .

A final area strongly affected by the media's anti-gun bias is that of accidental shootings. When it comes to this, reporters are eager to write about guns. Many have seen the public service ads showing the voices or pictures of children between the ages of four and eight, implying that there is an epidemic of accidental deaths of these young children.

Data I have collected show that accidental shooters overwhelmingly are adults with long histories of arrests for violent crimes, alcoholism, suspended or revoked drivers licenses, and involvement in car crashes. Meanwhile, the annual number of accidental gun deaths involving children under ten—most of these being cases where someone older shoots the child—is consistently a single digit number. It is a kind of media archetype story, to report on "naturally curious" children shooting themselves or other children—though from 1995 to 1999 the entire United States saw only between five and nine cases a year where a child under ten either accidentally shot themselves or another child.

Media bias against guns hurts society, and costs lives.

The danger of children stumbling across guns pales in comparison to many other risks. Over 1,260 children under ten died in cars in 1999. Another 370 died as pedestrians hit by cars. Accidents involving residential fires took 484 children's lives. Bicycles are much more likely to result in accidental deaths than guns. Fully 93 children under the age of ten drowned accidentally in bathtubs. Thirty-six children under five drowned in buckets during 1998. In fact, the number of children under ten who die from any type of accidental gunshot is smaller than the number of toddlers who drown in buckets. Yet few reporters crusade against buckets or bathtubs.

When crimes are committed with guns, there is a some-what natural inclination toward eliminating all guns. While understandable, this reaction actually endangers people's lives because it ignores how important guns are in protecting people from harm. Unbalanced media coverage exaggerates this, leaving most Americans with a glaringly incomplete picture of the dangers and benefits of firearms. This is how the media bias against guns hurts society, and costs lives.

4

America's Gun-Centered Culture Is Responsible for Mass Shootings

Robert Jay Lifton

Robert Jay Lifton is a lecturer in psychiatry at Harvard Medical School and professor emeritus of psychiatry at the City University of New York Graduate Center.

America's gun-centered culture plays a significant role in rampages such as the Virginia Tech shooting that left thirty-three people dead on April 16, 2007. In the United States guns are more than killing devices—the gun is an icon of American society. Guns are so much a part of American culture that even in the face of tragic school shootings, Americans are reluctant to suggest policies to control them. Indeed, guns are seen as a solution to social problems such as the madness of the Virginia Tech shooter. Some claim that the death toll could have been halted if students had been allowed to carry guns.

The combination of mental disease and access to guns leaps out at almost everyone in connection with the [April 16, 2007,] Virginia Tech shootings. But, from there, ideas and advocacies tend to become amorphous and tinged with hopelessness. There is consensus that something should be done to intervene earlier in threatening forms of psychological disturbance, and as a psychiatrist I agree and also recognize some of

Robert Jay Lifton, "An Ideology of 'Gunism,'" *Chronicle of Higher Education*, vol. 53, May 4, 2007, p. B11. Copyright © 2007 by The Chronicle of Higher Education. This article may not be published, reposted, or redistributed without express permission from *The Chronicle*.

the social obstacles to doing so. But while there will always be mentally ill people, a few of whom are violent, it is our gun-centered cultural disease that converts mental illness into massacre.

An Ideology of "Gunism"

Indeed, I would claim that a gun is not just a lethal device but a psychological actor in this terrible drama. Guns and ammunition were at the heart of [Virginia Tech shooter] Seung-Hui Cho's elaborate orchestration of the event and of his Rambo-like self-presentation to the world. When you look at those pictures [of Cho posing with guns], you understand how a gun can merge so fully with a person that a man who makes regular use of it could (in the historical West and in Hollywood) become known as a "gun."

American society, in the absence of an encompassing and stable traditional culture, has embraced the gun as a substitute . . . and created a vast cultural ideology we can call 'gunism.'

Some years ago, the distinguished historian Richard Hofstadter told me that, after a lifetime of studying American culture, what he found most deeply troubling was our country's inability to come to terms with the gun—which in turn strongly affected our domestic and international attitudes. Emotions of extreme attachment to and even sacralization of the gun pervade American society, and commercial interests shamelessly manipulate those emotions to produce wildly self-destructive policies.

Much has been said, with considerable truth, about the role of the frontier in bringing about this psychological condition. I would go further and suggest that American society, in the absence of an encompassing and stable traditional culture, has embraced the gun as a substitute for that absence, and created a vast cultural ideology we can call "gunism." Paradoxically, this highly destabilizing object became viewed as a baseline and an icon that could somehow sustain us in a new form of nontraditional society. That new society was to be democratic and egalitarian, so that the gun could be both an "equalizer," as it is sometimes known, and also a solution to various social problems. That idea of the gun as ultimate solution reached a kind of mad absurdity in [former Speaker of the House] Newt Gingrich's recent suggestion that university killings be prevented by having students carry hidden guns into classrooms. The gun as ultimate solution has also played a significant role in American military misadventures in Vietnam and Iraq, and in our attitudes toward nuclear weapons (as gigantic "guns").

With a problem so deep-seated, it is no wonder that suggestions of changing gun policies have been so readily dismissed as "an old story" (which unfortunately they are), as politically unfeasible, and as generally useless. But even deep-seated cultural patterns can be altered, and there is considerable support for altering this one. Indeed, America is a country in which change itself is a dominant cultural pattern. We need to make quick small changes and slower, more fundamental ones. But to do that, we require a diagnosis of our cultural disease.

A Weak Cultural Morality Can Be Blamed for Gun Crime

Kurt Williamsen

Kurt Williamsen is associate editor of the New American, *a publication of the John Birch Society, a conservative organization espousing limited government and biblical values.*

A nation's cultural morality is more likely to predict its rate of gun crime than its gun laws. Gun-control advocates often cite countries such as Japan, which has little gun violence, to defend the success of gun-control laws. However, studies show that social controls such as self-respect, honor, and conformity lead to Japan's low gun crime rate. In fact, as Japanese youth have become increasingly exposed to foreign influences, the violent crime rate has begun to climb. If the high rate of gun violence in the United States is indeed a reflection of its culture, banning guns will not protect Americans; it will only leave them unarmed.

The toll of the [April 16, 2007,] Virginia Tech shooting was 33 human beings dead and dozens of others injured. The loss of so many innocent youths to a madman was heartrending. Making matters worse, if that's possible, was the manner of their deaths. Some were found in defensive positions, instinctively trying to ward off bullets with their bare hands.

I reflected long about what could have been done to prevent this useless carnage and pain. As I reflected, I listened to news commentators such as Charles Gibson, Katie Couric,

Kurt Williamsen, "Beyond the Gun-Control Debate," *The New American*, vol. 23, May 28, 2007, pp. 17–21. Copyright © 2007 The New American. Reproduced by permission.

and Brian Ross ask questions about whether lax gun-control laws were to blame for this shooting. Each of them strongly implied that new gun-control laws are the answer.

"But," I thought at the risk of offending those media luminaries, "where they're placing the blame for this violence is at odds with the respondents of an April [2007] ABC News poll, who blamed popular culture."

When asked in that April poll to choose a "primary cause of gun violence, far more Americans blamed the effects of popular culture (40 percent) or the way parents raise their children (35 percent) than the availability of guns (18 percent). In no population does more than about a fourth cite the availability of guns as the chief cause of violence."

What if popular culture is to blame—or more specifically, what if a lack of cultural morality is to blame? If the poll respondents are on to something and guns are not to blame, it needs to be asked, "Can a correlation be shown between cultural morals and rates of violent crime—especially gun crime?" Let us see.

Cultural morality is hands-down a more reliable factor for predicting violence with guns than gun-control laws are.

Examining Gun-Control Countries

Three of the most important countries held up to prove that gun-control measures work are Japan, England, and Australia. These countries' restrictive laws against civilians owning guns, which make owning a gun for defensive purposes either difficult or nearly impossible, are credited with producing much lower rates of gun deaths in those countries than in America. Assuming the lower death rates are true, it must only be learned whether the lower reported deaths are owing to gun control or culture.

The results of my perusal of the research on this topic were conclusive: cultural morality is hands-down a more reliable factor for predicting violence with guns than gun-control laws are.

Japan: Japan has both very strict gun-control laws and a very low number of shootings each year, yet the gun-control laws don't seem to play a major role in reducing violence and deaths. In Japan, only a tiny fraction of people may own handguns, and the owners of rifles and shotguns must pass several tests to acquire a gun and then they must keep the guns in a locker at home. . . . *Time* magazine reported that there were only 53 shootings there in 2006 in a population of just over 127 million. A pretty good record in anyone's book.

But researcher David B. Kopel pointed out in a 1993 article for the *Asia Pacific Law Review*, entitled "Japanese Gun Control," that "more than gun control, more than the lack of criminal procedure safeguards, more than the authority of the police, it is the pervasive social controls that best explain the low crime rate." In his article, Kopel explains, "Almost everyone [in Japan] accepts the paradigm that the police should be respected. Because the police are so esteemed, the Japanese people co-operate with the police more than Americans do. Co-operation with the police also extends to obeying laws which almost everyone believes in. The Japanese people, and even the large majority of Japanese criminals, voluntarily obey gun controls."

In fact, Japanese police visit the home of each Japanese citizen twice each year to update the extensive dossiers that they keep on each Japanese citizen. The dossiers are so inclusive that they even list the reasons teen girls give for having sex.

The Impact of Japanese Culture

Kopel explained that Japanese culture is all about tradition, conforming, joining, self-respect, and honor—not about individuality and self-gratification. "When Japanese parents punish their children," Kopel asserted, "they do not make the children stay inside the house, as American parents do. Punishment for a Japanese child means being put outside. The sublimation of individual desires to the greater good, the pressure to conform, and internalised willingness to do so are much stronger in Japan than in America."

It is the uniqueness of Japanese conformity that lends itself to low crime rates, not gun control.

Kopel provides much evidence to back up his assertion that it is the uniqueness of Japanese conformity that lends itself to low crime rates, not gun control: suicide rates in Japan are double those in America (Japanese who can't conform often kill themselves); the former Soviet Union had strict gun-control laws and onerous controls on the people but high violent-crime rates; the non-gun robbery rates in Japan were also low (70 times lower than the rate in America); and even Japanese prisons had extremely low rates of violence—especially when compared to America.

Additionally, as the Japanese culture has changed, so too has the crime rate, which has been moving up despite the fact that the gun laws are still in place. Violent crime in Japan has been climbing as the Japanese have been increasingly exposed to foreign influences from both media and the masses of legal and illegal immigrants who have entered the country. Back in 1993, Kopel reported that "per one million inhabitants, Tokyo has 40 reported muggings a year, New York has 11,000." Ten years later, a 2003 article in *Japan Today* reported on increasingly prevalent and violent crimes by teenagers in Japan "known as 'Oyajigari' (literally, old man hunting)" and "'hatsuden-nerai' (aiming for the first train)"—teens armed with baseball bats and martial-arts weapons attacking and robbing old men and businessmen.

A separate report on PBS's *Nightly Business Report* revealed that "the number of juveniles indicted for serious crimes such as murder and rape and armed robbery soared 51.3 percent in 1997" and "the growth of robberies and thefts rose by 50,000 in 2000—a total of 385,717."

England and Violent Crime

Japan's experience with violent crime increasing despite great restrictions on guns is not an anomaly; England followed the same path, to the great sorrow of many of her citizens.

The explanation for . . . low crime rates must . . . be found in the British culture, not the gun-control laws.

Are the reports about Britain's low crime a big lie? The answer is that England did once have low crime rates, but the low rates had already existed prior to the introduction of gun-control laws. The explanation for those low crime rates must therefore be found in the British culture, not the gun-control laws. According to a 2002 article in *Reason* magazine, "A government study [in England] for the years 1890–92 . . . found only three handgun homicides, an average of one a year, in a population of 30 million. In 1904 there were only four armed robberies in London, then the largest city in the world." At the time, guns were prevalent in English society. These low rates lasted until about 1954 when rates of violent crime began to creep upwards. *Reason* magazine reported that in recent years "armed crime, with banned handguns the weapon of choice, was 'rocketing.' In the two years following the 1997 handgun ban, the use of handguns in crime rose by 40 percent, and the upward trend has continued. From April to November 2001, the number of people robbed at gunpoint in London rose 53 percent."

In September 2005, 18-year-old Ruth Okechukwu was dragged from her car in south London and stabbed repeatedly; she died. Fifteen days earlier, the killer, Roberto Malasi, had also killed Zainab Kalokoh at a baby-christening party, shooting her in the head, before robbing the guests of their valuables. Such behavior has been on an upward trend.

[Anchorman] Dan Rather reported on CBS News in 2000 that Great Britain had become "one of the most violent urban societies in the Western world." This in a country where, according to the National Rifle Association, "licenses have been required for rifles and handguns since 1920, and for shotguns since 1967. A decade ago semiautomatic and pump-action center-fire rifles, and all handguns except single-shot .22s, were prohibited. The .22s were banned in 1997."

Reason magazine further illuminated Great Britain's crime problems: "Except for murder and rape, . . . 'Britain has overtaken the US for all major crimes,'" it said, quoting the *Mirror* of London. *Reason* added: "In the two years since Dan Rather" made public England's crime problem, "violence in England has gotten markedly worse. Over the course of a few days in the summer of 2001, gun-toting men burst into an English court and freed two defendants; a shooting outside a London nightclub left five women and three men wounded, and two men were machine-gunned to death in a residential neighborhood of North London. And on New Year's day [in 2007] a 19-year-old girl walking on a main street in east London was shot in the head by a thief who wanted her mobile phone."

Reason went on: "In reality, the English approach has not reduced violent crime. Instead it has left law-abiding citizens at the mercy of criminals who are confident that their victims have neither the means nor the legal right to resist them. Initiating this model would be a public safety disaster for the United States." In England robbers are so confident of having defenseless victims that "53 percent of English burglaries occur while the occupants are at home, compared with 13 percent in the US, where burglars admit to fearing armed homeowners more than police."

Despite the UK's [United Kingdom's] restrictive weapons-control policies and their pervasive monitoring of the public through closed-circuit cameras, crimes committed with guns and knives are flourishing. The BBC News reported: "In 2003, there were 31 youths aged under 20 charged with gun-related murder in London. In 2006, interim figures showed that number had risen to 76."

Theories behind [England's] low crime rates ... all have one thing in common: cultural morality.

Simply put, for many years before gun laws were enacted, the English for some reason seldom committed crimes. Theories behind such low crime rates range from prior centuries of strict punishment for crimes—frequent hangings—to religious devotion to extremely nationalistic English pride and propriety, but they all have one thing in common: cultural morality.

Trends in Australia

Australia had the same disconcerting result when it instituted severe gun restrictions. In March 2006, the *Sydney Morning Herald* reported that of the 30 developed countries in the Organization for Economic Cooperation and Development, "Australia had the highest proportion of victims of assaults, threats and crimes of a sexual nature, the second highest proportion of burglaries, and high rates of robberies, car thefts and thefts from cars. . . . The US, which recorded a fall in victimization rates, was mid-range." And if you remember, Australia prohibited many semiautomatic and pump rifles and shotguns in 1996, and it requires that each gun owner be able to verify a "Genuine Reason" for obtaining a gun, and self-defense is not considered a genuine reason.

Summed up, though the number of homicides committed with guns did go down to 17 percent of all homicides in 2003–04—a continuing trend that began in 1969, well before the enactment of strict gun-control measures—the number of homicides in the country spiked in 1999, three years after strict gun-control measures went into effect. Armed robbery and unarmed robbery both peaked in March 2001. The trend in assaults shows a continuing increase, with "an average growth of 6 percent each year between 1995 and 2003," according to the Australian Institute of Criminology Similarly, sexual assaults "have increased by an average 4 percent each year since 1995." . . .

Crime Rates in the United States

Here in America, there are currently 36 shall-issue states— states that will issue a concealed-carry permit to those citizens who pass the required background checks and gun training— and 10 states that allow at least some semblance of right-to-carry. Before these concealed-carry laws were passed, anti-gunners predicted their passage would lead to huge spikes in violent crime. Those spikes didn't happen. According to a Fox News column in March [2007], "The violent crime rate fell for 13 straight years, a total drop of 39 percent, before increasing in 2005 by less than 1 percent. . . . Murder rates have essentially remained unchanged since 2000 after falling from a peak of 9.8 in 1991."

[The] present high murder rate [in the United States] is a reflection of our culture, not guns.

What does all of this mean for us here in the United States? Strict gun-control laws, including banning guns, will likely lead to an increase in murders and other violent crime here because our present high murder rate is a reflection of our culture, not guns, and because the law-abiding would then be largely disarmed.

Addressing the Problem

Can we use this knowledge to reduce crime in a society that almost worships cultural diversity, rather than promoting cultural unity; and in a society where "gangsta rap" regularly glorifies the killing of other races and of police officers; and in a society where the races and social strati are pitted against one another by affirmative action laws and so-called hate-crime laws? That remains to be seen.

As David C. Stolinsky, M.D., said in a brief analysis of the cause and amount of crime in the United States entitled "America: The Most Violent Nation?": "We all must admit that we have much to learn about the causes of violence. This requires more effort and intellectual honesty than looking to government to pass yet another law. America is hardly the most violent nation, and our homicide rate has fallen recently, but we are more violent than we used to be—and than we should be."

However, even by remedying our culture, we cannot completely solve the problem as was demonstrated in Japan in 2001 when Mamoru Takuma entered an elementary school in Osaka, then used a kitchen knife to kill eight students and wound 15 other people. There will always be immoral people, but we can ameliorate the problem.

Taking away guns from the law-abiding, as our survey shows, will not change what's in our hearts, but will make us more vulnerable.

6

A Lack of Gun Control Leads to Gun Crime

Lillian B. Rubin

Lillian B. Rubin is a sociologist, psychologist, and author of numerous books, including 60 On Up: The Truth About Aging in America.

Only eliminating access to guns in America can prevent mass murders such as the shooting rampage that left thirty-three people dead at Virginia Tech on April 16, 2007. Nevertheless, rather than accept that guns kill, which is indeed what guns are designed to do, people find it easier to blame the family, mental health professionals, and even society for tragic mass shootings. Strengthening family values, increasing the influence of the church, or meeting the difficult challenge of identifying potentially violent individuals, however, will not be as effective as simply preventing a killer's access to guns.

Dawn broke on April 16, 2007, as it does always, but this day would soon reveal itself to be unlike any other. For this was the day that a twenty-three-year-old student walked onto the campus at Virginia Tech carrying two semi-automatic pistols—a Glock 9 mm and a Walther P22—and fired close to two hundred rounds, killing thirty-two people and injuring scores more in the deadliest shooting rampage in our nation's history. Minutes later, long before anyone knew any of the facts, reporters filled the airwaves, the Web buzzed with headlines, and the show was on—a spectacle nearly as obscene as the massacre itself.

Analyzing the Shooter

As reporters dug for the story behind the killing spree and found that the shooter, Cho Seung-Hui, had been ordered by a judge to undergo outpatient treatment after he was diagnosed in December 2005 as "mentally ill and in need of hospitalization," the din increased, and the psychology of the killer moved to center stage. Nearly every news show featured its very own mental health "expert"—psychologists and psychiatrists, none of whom had ever met Cho Seung-Hui and knew almost nothing about him, yet had no problem offering up instant, and often contradictory, psychological analyses to explain why he did it. Having spent over three decades of my professional life in clinical practice and knowing its uncertainties, I wondered how these guys (and they were almost always "guys") dared to speak with such assurance, as if psychology were a mathematics-like science where it's perfectly clear that if you add two and two, you will always get four. It's as if they had a recipe: pour a little anger into the pot, mix well with violent fantasies, add a big dollop of alienation, and you'll have yourself a mass murderer. Sounds like a lot of teenagers and young adults we all know, doesn't it?

I listened to my local public radio station most of that day, then turned to various television news programs during the evening, waiting in vain for one of these experts to acknowledge that, whatever Cho's psychological state, he couldn't have killed and injured so many people if he hadn't had two semi-automatic weapons in his hands. Instead, I heard an orgy of blame.

Looking for Someone to Blame

Because the theory to which most mental health professionals have dedicated their lives tells them that the seeds of the son's problems must lie in the family, the parents were at the top of the list. This must be a seriously dysfunctional family, they announced. Didn't these people talk to their son? How could they not have known that this young man was so troubled? Never mind that the parents had tried unsuccessfully to get help for their son, and that this was widely reported. Never mind, either, the obvious fact that whatever our individual differences may be, our psychology is born and takes root in a social environment whose reach is well beyond the bounds of family, an environment in which it is all too easy to get the guns to carry out the violent fantasies. Theory trumped fact.

If not the family, who else to blame? The school officials, obviously. Why didn't they intervene when they saw earlier signs that he was a troubled young man? Why, when two people were shot dead two hours before the massacre, didn't they lock down the campus? Good questions, but they still avoid the central one: how is it possible to protect against this kind of mass violence in a society where such a vast number of guns circulate so freely?

The professors, too, got their share of blame. Why didn't they take more seriously the rage and violence he expressed in written assignments? But real life doesn't mimic television, and unlike the show in which FBI profilers always catch their prey because they can accurately assess "the criminal mind," it's virtually impossible for even the professionally trained to predict when a young person's violent and/or suicidal fantasies are anything more than an outlet for blowing off steam.

Counseling the Traumatized

Meanwhile, in the midst of all the talk, the grief counselors were gathering, ready to "help" the students, teachers, and their families through the trauma and teach them to express their grief and rage "constructively." Plug grief counseling into Google and you come up with 1.2 million hits and what seems like an endless list of professionals and organizations offering what one Web site calls "the uncharted waters of the grieving process." Uncharted waters? It has been nearly forty years since the five stages of grief—denial, anger, bargaining, depression, and acceptance—as laid out by Elisabeth Kubler-Ross entered public consciousness to become the basis for a burgeoning grief industry, in which mental health professionals of all stripes counsel people on how to do it right, as if they hadn't been grieving without a map since the beginning of time.

I'm not arguing for or against the idea of stages of grief, although my experience as a psychotherapist warns me against taking as gospel any notion that lays out a series of universal steps necessary to complete or resolve any psychological process. Kubler-Ross's five stages make some intellectual sense. Whether they make emotional sense for all or even most people is quite another question—one few mental health professionals ask.

People couldn't kill on a mass scale without guns.

The Social Context

So what's wrong with all the psychologizing if it helps us understand such tragic events better, gets us through the grieving process a little easier? What's wrong is that it focuses entirely on the individual, with little or no attempt to put that behavior into its social context. What's wrong is that it assumes that if we understand the psychology, we can change the behavior and save ourselves from future atrocities like Virginia Tech or Columbine [High School in Colorado, where in 1999 two students killed thirteen and themselves] or the shootings in various post offices and corporate headquarters in recent years. But that isn't true. Despite the National Rifle Association's insistence that "Guns don't kill people, people kill people," people couldn't kill on a mass scale without guns.

Yes, I know, guns aren't the only culprits in violent assaults. And I know, too, that we need to do better in identifying people like Cho Seung-Hui before they wreak their havoc.

But we already know that we won't always be able to do this, that there will probably be a next person and a next who is troubled enough to exact his revenge (and it is, so far, almost always a "he") on some community for real or imagined slights. The question now is, will he have access to guns, our uniquely American weapon of mass destruction, that will allow him to kill scores of people in a few minutes?

Look at the statistics. In a single year, close to 20,000 Americans suffer nonfatal gun injuries, while 34,000 more, including over 3,000 children and teenagers, are killed by gunfire. That's one child killed every three hours, nine children every day, and more than sixty children every week. In the same year not a single Japanese child died of gunshot wounds, Great Britain had 19 deaths, Germany 57, France 109, and Canada 153.

In the aftermath of the Virginia Tech murders, we've had a litany of suggestions for prevention, almost all of them focused on individual behavior, with the exception of the favored bogeyman: television and film violence. I'm not suggesting that we should be complacent about the violence that's so plentiful in our media or that the incivility and vulgarity so prominent in our culture today isn't worthy of comment and discussion. But appeals to strengthening family values, more religious training and involvement in church, and early identification of potentially violent individuals are truly, as [folk singer] Bob Dylan would have it, "blowin' in the wind."

Eliminating Guns

Although any or all of the suggested interventions may have some value, they will not by themselves eliminate the mass shootings in schools or the thirty-odd thousand deaths by gunfire outside the schoolyard. Only eliminating guns will do the job. And I don't mean just closing the loopholes in laws we already know don't work or promulgating new ones that will just as easily be subverted. I'm speaking of federal and state laws that will take the existing stockpile of two hundred million guns out of the hands of ordinary citizens and ban the further sale and possession of handguns except for people who have some legitimate, professional reason to carry them.

Ah, yes, I forgot for a moment: there's that pesky Second Amendment to the Bill of Rights that declares, "A well regulated militia, being necessary to the security of a free state, the right of the people to keep and bear arms, shall not be infringed." These twenty-seven words continue to be the historical justification for millions of guns in private hands. I'm not a constitutional lawyer and not qualified to join the esoteric debate about what the framers meant when they wrote these words. But then, whether opponents of gun control or proponents, they don't know either; it's all speculation based on the political/social philosophy that's dominant at any given time.

No spin by those stalwarts who insist on our right to carry guns can change the fact that their unregulated use has unleashed a murderous plague.

What I do know is that the Bill of Rights was ratified in 1791, when this country was still in need of its "well regulated militia" to ensure the security of its new and untried government. What does that have to do with handguns owned and used today by ordinary citizens who are not part of any organized militias? Or with a powerful government whose "security as a free state" is not in question, at least not from its own people?

It's time to put an end to the arguments about the meaning of the Second Amendment and come to terms with the social and political realities of the twenty-first century. Guns kill; it's what they're meant to do. And no spin by those stalwarts who insist on our right to carry guns can change the fact that their unregulated use has unleashed a murderous plague that kills and injures far too many victims every year.

Yes, people will continue to kill each other even if we ban guns. But all the evidence, not to mention plain common sense, tells us that they can't do it so efficiently and in such large numbers without the aid of a gun.

7

Gun Control Does Not Reduce Violent Crime

Richard A. Levy

Richard A. Levy is a senior fellow in constitutional studies at the Cato Institute, a libertarian think tank in Washinton, D.C.

There is no evidence that gun-control laws reduce violent crime, suicide, or accidents. Indeed, gun-control laws failed to stop the crazed gunman who took the lives of thirty-two people before killing himself at Virginia Tech on April 16, 2007. Studies show that guns are used defensively more often than they are used to commit crimes. Gun control does little to reduce crime, and it prevents innocent victims from defending themselves against predators.

"What is needed, urgently, is stronger controls over the lethal weapons that cause such wasteful carnage." So said the *New York Times* in its predictable but wrongheaded editorial the day after the horrific events at Virginia Tech. Anti-gun advocates, however noble their motives, help create the environment in which horrors like [the April 16, 2007, shooting rampage at] Virginia Tech occur.

No spin by those stalwarts who insist on our right to carry guns can change the fact that their unregulated use has unleashed a murderous plague.

Possession and use of guns on the Tech campus violated state-imposed restrictions. But crazed fanatics, undeterred by

Richard A. Levy, "They Never Learn," *American Spectator*, April 25, 2007. Reproduced by permission.

laws against murder, will not be dissuaded by laws against guns. More such laws will accomplish nothing. Indeed, liberalized laws might have enabled responsible, armed citizens on campus to defend the hapless victims. It took two hours for the killer methodically to massacre 32 people and injure another 15. Why did nobody intervene sooner to stop the killer?

No Right to Carry Handguns

For one possible explanation, consider this report from a *Roanoke Times* article: A bill, introduced on behalf of the Virginia Citizens Defense League, would have given properly licensed public college students and employees the right to carry handguns on campus. The bill died on January 30, 2006 in the Virginia General Assembly. Virginia Tech spokesman Larry Hincker was pleased with the outcome. "I'm sure the university community is appreciative of the General Assembly's actions because this will help parents, students, faculty and visitors feel safe on our campus." Tell that to the ill-fated victims of April 16 and their families.

The article goes on to relate that most universities in Virginia require students and employees, other than police, to check their guns with police or campus security on entering campus. The proposed legislation would have eliminated that requirement for anyone who possessed a valid concealed handgun permit. Ironically, Tech's governing board had approved in June 2005 a violence prevention policy reiterating the school's ban on students, employees, or visitors—even those properly licensed—from bringing handguns onto campus.

At the Virginia Tech press conference after the slaughter of 32 defenseless people, the university's president cautioned that it wouldn't be possible to have police guard every classroom and dorm. What he omitted was this cold, hard fact: By making the university a "gun free zone," his administration and the state legislature had fostered a climate in which ubiquitous police would be necessary. Without a means to protect themselves, Virginia Tech students, faculty, and other employees were more likely to be victimized by the only people on campus who had readily available guns: killers and lunatics.

Gun control does not work. It just prevents weaker people from defending themselves against stronger predators.

Gun Control Does Not Work

Meanwhile, the *New York Times*, the Brady Center [to Prevent Gun Violence, founded by former White House press secretary and gun violence victim James Brady], and the rest of the usual suspects continue their clamor for more gun regulations—apparently oblivious to the destructive effects of their own proposals. The evidence is clear: more guns in the hands of responsible owners yield lower rates of violent crime. Gun control does not work. It just prevents weaker people from defending themselves against stronger predators.

Here are the numbers, as summarized by legal scholar Don B. Kates: Over the 30-year period from 1974 to 2003, guns in circulation doubled, but murder rates declined by a third. On a state-by-state basis, a 1 percent increase in gun ownership correlates with a 4.1 percent lower rate of violent crime. Each year, approximately 460,000 gun crimes are committed in the United States. But guns are also used to ward off gun criminals. Estimates of defensive gun use range from 1.3 million to 2.5 million times per year—and usually the weapons are merely brandished, not fired. That means defensive uses occur about 3-to-5 times as often as violent gun crimes. Just as important, *armed* victims who resist gun criminals get injured less frequently than *unarmed* victims who submit. In more than 8 out of 10 cases where the victim pulls a gun, the criminal turns and flees, even if he's armed. "So much for the quasi-religious faith that more guns mean more murder."

Finally, two federal government agencies recently examined gun control laws and found no statistically significant evidence to support their effectiveness. In 2004, the National Academy of Sciences reviewed 253 journal articles, 99 books, and 43 government publications evaluating 80 gun-control measures. The researchers could not identify a single gun-control regulation that reduced violent crime, suicide, or accidents. A year earlier, the Centers for Disease Control and Prevention reported on an independent evaluation of firearms and ammunition bans, restrictions on acquisition, waiting periods, registration, licensing, child access prevention laws, and zero tolerance laws. Conclusion: none of the laws had a meaningful impact on gun violence.

When will the gun controllers learn?

8

The Increased Availability of Guns Reduces Crime

John Luik

John Luik, a Canadian philosopher and health policy analyst, has worked at several conservative Canadian think tanks, including the Niagara and Fraser institutes.

Studies show that the chance of being the victim of a violent crime decreases as the availability of guns increases. In fact, citizens with guns have thwarted several potentially tragic school shootings. Laws banning guns will not, therefore, protect people. Indeed, Virginia Tech's campus gun ban was unable to protect the students murdered there on April 16, 2007.

[In early May 2007], a Grade 9 student in Calgary [Alberta, Canada] confessed to his parents he was planning to carry out an attack on some of his teachers on the April 20 anniversary of the 1999 Columbine massacre [in Colorado, in which fifteen died]. Then came the [April 16, 2007,] tragedy at Virginia Polytechnic Institute and State University [Virginia Tech]. Invariably, in these circumstances, the talk in Canada and the U.S. turns to gun control.

Among the first off the mark was California Senator Dianne Feinstein, who said, "It is my deep belief that shootings like these are enabled by the unparalleled ease with which people procure weapons in this country." Feinstein, who has had a concealed-handgun permit herself, was quickly followed

John Luik, "Bulletproofing Canada: Gun Control Won't Prevent School Shootings. But Having Guns Might Help Individuals Mitigate Them," *Western Standard*, May 21, 2007, pp. 41–45. Copyright © 2007 Western Standard. Reproduced by permission.

by presidential candidate John Edwards, who opined that the Virginia shooting showed the need for new gun restrictions. Indeed, the subtext for much of the media coverage of the Virginia Tech story, both in Canada and the U.S., was that bulletproofing the United States from subsequent carnage requires tough new controls on guns.

Canadians often feel unjustifiably smug about the "effectiveness" of gun control here versus in the U.S. But research has shown that even with widely differing gun ownership rates and regulations, neighbouring Canadian and U.S communities that are socially, economically and demographically alike have similar homicide rates.

The chances of innocent people being the victims of violent crime, including murder, decrease—not increase—when access to guns is made easier.

Looking at the Evidence

If the evidence suggests anything about gun control, it is that the chances of innocent people being the victims of violent crime, including murder, decrease—not increase—when access to guns is made easier. The more people who own guns, the less violent crime there is. The evidence for this comes in a number of forms, most definitively in John Lott's massive study of guns and crime in the U.S. from 1977 to 1996, titled *More Guns, Less Crime.*

Lott's question was whether allowing people to carry concealed handguns deters violent crime. His assumption was that criminals are rational in that their reaction to an increase in the number of armed potential victims is to commit fewer crimes. Lott looked at the FBI's crime statistics for all 3,054 U.S. counties. He found that, over the period of his study, gun ownership had been increasing across the country—from 27.4 per cent in 1988 to 37 per cent by 1996—yet crime rates had been falling. More specifically, states with the greatest decrease in crime rates were those with the fastest increases in gun ownership.

According to Lott, for each additional year that laws allowing people to carry concealed handguns were on the books, robberies declined by two per cent, rapes by two per cent and murders by three per cent. If all states that did not permit carrying concealed handguns had allowed them in 1992, for instance, there would have been 1,839 fewer murders, 3,727 rapes and 10,990 aggravated assaults.

Allowing Access to Guns

The importance of allowing citizens access to guns as a life-saving measure is even more evident when it comes to instances of multiple-victim public shootings at schools. Lott, for instance, looks at the eight public-school shootings that occurred from 1997 to 2000. In two of these cases—Pearl, Miss., and Edinboro, Pa.—the attacks were stopped by citizens with guns. Interestingly, as Lott notes in his 2003 book, *The Bias Against Guns*, during Virginia's other university shooting, at the Appalachian School of Law in January 2002, it was three students, two of them armed, who overcame the attacker and prevented further killing.

Lott and co-researcher William Landes also looked at all multiple-victim public shootings in the U.S. from 1977 to 1995. Over this period, 14 states adopted right-to-carry gun laws, and the number of such shootings declined by 84 per cent, with deaths in the shootings reduced by 90 per cent.

It is sadly ironic that the Virginia Tech story might have been different if a bill to prohibit so-called "gun-free zones," such as the one at Virginia Tech, had passed the Virginia General Assembly in [2006]. That legislation was drafted to prevent state universities like Virginia Tech from prohibiting students with concealed handgun permits from carrying guns on campus.

Once the grieving has abated, there will be time to look at the events at Virginia Tech more through the lens of policy and less through emotion. Then we will find that, while it is clear no government policy could have prevented such horrible sadness, it is equally clear that allowing people to carry guns was not the real cause.

9

The Claim That Increased Gun Availability Reduces Crime Is Unfounded

Sabina Thaler

Sabina Thaler is a 2007 graduate of Virginia Tech who lives in Roanoke, Virginia.

Several flaws have been found in the oft-cited theory that communities where people are allowed to carry concealed weapons experience lower crime rates. John Lott and David Mustard's premise that crime victims uniformly use guns in self-defense is false. Women, for example, are less likely to use guns to protect themselves and are in fact in greater danger when doing so. Moreover, critics of Lott and Mustard's research found that when using actual crime data, in the rare instance when increased gun availability does lead to less crime, the difference is not significant.

Joe Painter presented a compelling challenge in the June 14 [2007] issue of *The Roanoke Times*.

By way of a specific scientific analysis, Painter hypothesized that more guns equal less crime. Because I love a good debate, and because I believe my rights to not be searched or shot are greater than your right to bear arms, I am accepting this challenge.

While Painter develops an excellent hypothesis, he commits the serious fallacy of approaching the data from the perspective of a lawyer as opposed to that of a scientist. The difference between lawyers and scientists is that lawyers seek to prove their side right; whereas, scientists go to great lengths to prove they're wrong.

I admit John Lott and David Mustard's data, to which Painter refers, sound convincing. Indeed, if these results are accurate we can no longer find irony with conservatives who are simultaneously pro-life and pro-gun.

A Study Plagued with Errors

Luckily for the challenge at hand, Lott and Mustard's study is plagued with errors. For one, this study relies on the premise that guns are uniformly used for protection. In other words, when using a gun defensively, a person will behave the same regardless of his or her age, sex, social status, gang affiliation, etc.

If this seems plausible, read Stephen Schnebly's analysis of the impact of the victim on defensive gun use. Schnebly finds that victims behave differently when using a gun for protection. A woman is much less likely to fire a gun in defending herself than is a man. In fact, with the exception of domestic situations, statistically a woman is in more danger if she attempts to use a firearm to protect herself than she would be without a gun.

Readers might be thinking: "Schnebly's theory does not necessarily disprove Lott and Mustard's theory. Couldn't there still be a chance that, even when controlling for this disparity, guns will prove their superior powers of crime control?"

No.

In 1998 two scientists, Hashem Dezhbakhsh and Paul Rubin, sensed something fishy with Lott and Mustard's study. Dezhbakhsh and Rubin decided to see what would happen if they replaced Lott and Mustard's "dummy" variables with the crime rate that actually occurred. To the National Rifle

Association's dismay, they found that Lott and Mustard's theory did not hold up in the real world.

Concealed gun laws are correlated with an increase in crime; for those few instances where guns are correlated with lessened crime, the difference is much less significant.

In many cases, Lott and Mustard's concealed gun laws are correlated with an increase in crime; for those few instances where guns are correlated with lessened crime, the difference is much less significant than Lott and Mustard theorized. The reason people don't tout Lott and Mustard's analysis is because it was based on several problematic assumptions that ultimately devastated and discredited their findings.

Crime is almost certainly caused by multiple factors. Guns should not be America's whipping boy. Nevertheless, guns make taking lives too easy. We cannot identify and detain every potential criminal; but, by eliminating firearms, we will make it much more difficult for robbers to become murderers.

10

Concealed-Carry Laws Make People Safer

Michael Barone

Michael Barone is a senior writer with U.S. News & World Report, *a weekly newsmagazine.*

People are safer in states where law-abiding citizens are allowed to carry concealed weapons. Fears that such states would become shooting galleries have proven to be unfounded. Banning weapons does not guarantee safety. After all, people at gun-free Virginia Tech, where more than thirty were killed by a student gunman in 2007, were not safe. Law-abiding citizens on campuses with no ban on carrying concealed weapons, however, have been able to halt shooting rampages. While reasonable regulations that prevent guns from getting into the wrong hands are necessary, people are safer when allowed to carry weapons.

The murders [on April 16, 2007,] at Virginia Tech naturally set off a cry in the usual quarters—the *New York Times*, the London-based *Economist*—for stricter gun control laws. Democratic officeholders didn't chime in, primarily because they believe they were hurt by the issue in 2000 and 2004, but most privately agree.

Two Tracks of Debate

What most discussions of this issue tend to ignore is that we have two tracks of political debate and two sets of laws on gun control. At the federal level there has been a push for more gun control laws since [President] John Kennedy was assassinated in 1963, and some modest restrictions have been passed. At the state level something entirely different has taken place. In 1987 Florida passed a law allowing citizens who could demonstrate that they were law-abiding and had sufficient training to obtain permits on demand to own and carry concealed weapons. In the succeeding 20 years many other states have passed such laws, so that today you can, if you meet the qualifications, carry concealed weapons in 40 states with 67 percent of the nation's population (including Vermont, with no gun restrictions at all).

When Florida passed its concealed-weapons law, I thought it was a terrible idea. People would start shooting each other over traffic altercations; parking lots would turn into shooting galleries. Not so, it turned out. Only a very, very few concealed-weapons permits have been revoked. There are only rare incidents in which people with concealed-weapons permits have used them unlawfully. Ordinary law-abiding people, it turns out, are pretty trustworthy.

In places where gun ownership is widespread, we're safer than in a 'gun-free zone.'

Unfounded Fears

I'm not the only one to draw such a conclusion. When she was Michigan's attorney general, Democrat Jennifer Granholm opposed the state's concealed-weapons law, which took effect in 2001. But now, as governor, she's not seeking its repeal. She says that her fears—like those I had about Florida's law 20 years ago—proved to be unfounded. So far as I know, there are no politically serious moves to repeal any state's concealed-weapons laws. In most of the United States, as you go to work, shop at the mall, go to restaurants, and walk around your neighborhood, you do so knowing that some of the people you pass by may be carrying a gun. You may not even think about it. But that's all right. Experience has shown that these people aren't threats.

Virginia has a concealed-weapons law. But Virginia Tech was, by the decree of its administrators, a "gun-free zone." Those with concealed-weapons permits were not allowed to take their guns on campus and were disciplined when they did. A bill was introduced in the House of Delegates to allow permit holders to carry guns on campus. When it was sidetracked, a Virginia Tech administrator hailed the action and said that students, professors, and visitors would now "feel safe" on campus. Tragically, they weren't safe. Virginia Tech's "gun-free zone" was not gun free. In contrast, killers on other campuses were stopped by faculty or bystanders who had concealed-weapons permits and brandished their guns to stop the killing.

We may hear more about gun control at the national level. The D.C. Circuit Court of Appeals recently ruled that the District of Columbia's ban on handguns violates the Second Amendment's right "to keep and bear arms." Judge Laurence Silberman's strong opinion argues that this is consistent with the Supreme Court's ruling in a 1939 case upholding a federal law banning sawed-off shotguns; limited regulation is allowed, Silberman wrote, but not a total ban. Somewhere on the road between a law banning possession of nuclear weapons and banning all guns the Second Amendment stands in the way. This is the view as well of the liberal constitutional law scholar Laurence Tribe. The Supreme Court may take the case, which is in conflict with other circuits' rulings.[The Court did agree to review the case in November 2007.]

If it upholds the D.C. decision, there is still room for reasonable gun regulation. The mental health ruling on the Virginia Tech killer surely should have been entered into the instant check database to prevent him from buying guns. The National Rifle Association is working with gun control advocate Rep. Carolyn McCarthy to improve that database. But even as we fine-tune laws to make sure guns don't get into the wrong hands, maybe the opinion elites will realize that in places where gun ownership is widespread, we're safer than in a "gun-free zone."

11

The Gun Industry Uses Fear to Promote Unnecessary Concealed-Carry Laws

Kris Berggren

Kris Berggren writes for the National Catholic Reporter, *an independent newsweekly that reflects and comments on the Roman Catholic Church and society.*

Despite knowing that people are killed by guns both intentionally and unintentionally, many Americans nevertheless believe that carrying a gun is necessary to protect themselves from uncertain threats to their safety. To encourage people to buy guns, the gun industry takes advantage of these latent fears. Women who fear being raped and ex-urban dwellers who fear being mugged on city streets are led to believe that they are safer carrying a gun. However, simply carrying a gun does not mean that people are safer or that they know when they may use the weapon legally.

In my home hangs a print called "Jesus Breaking the Rifle," by a German artist named Otto Pankok, which I bought a dozen years ago at Chicago's Peace Museum. It depicts Jesus in black and white, snapping a rifle across his knee as if it were a stick. It reminds my children and visitors that Jesus used words, not weapons, to solve problems and bridge differences between people.

Kris Berggren, "Fear-Rooted Gun Culture Kills Before Shot Is Fired," *National Catholic Reporter*, vol. 39, June 6, 2003, p. 18. Copyright © 2003 The National Catholic Reporter Publishing Company, 115 E. Armour Blvd., Kansas City, MO 64111. All rights reserved. Reproduced by permission of National Catholic Reporter, www.natcath.org.

Here's a Zen question for you: If a gun is locked in a cabinet, does anybody die? I suppose it's literally true that guns don't kill people; people kill people. But to be precise, people with guns kill people—and kill themselves, and cause unintentional injury and death.

Gun Culture Creep

I have long been anti-gun. I'm not really talking about hunting rifles, though I do admit that the allure of hunting as a sport escapes me. No, I'm talking about gun culture creep: what strikes me as a mood of increasing resignation on the part of the American people that guns are a necessary evil, a last resort of self-protection in a world that threatens their personal safety. The gun industry and its public relations arm, the National Rifle Association [NRA], are masterful marketers who take advantage of our latent anxieties, whether they're about specific things like a spate of crime in our neighborhoods, or uncertainties like the threat of foreign terrorists.

The proliferation of guns in our homes and public places reflects a deep-rooted fear that kills something in our souls before a shot is ever fired.

When I lived in Detroit I attended a weekly prayer vigil in the center of the downtown area organized by the Anti-Handgun Association. A co-worker in my building one day questioned my rationale for opposing guns. She told me of her parents' mom-and-pop grocery on a corner of a street in our often-lawless city. Because the store had been robbed before, she feared for her dad's life and was grateful that he owned a gun. I had to respect her experience, but it didn't change my core belief that the proliferation of guns in our homes and public places reflects a deep-rooted fear that kills something in our souls before a shot is ever fired.

My children wanted to know whether a permit to carry a gun also gives the gun owner permission to shoot someone. I explained that no, just because someone may carry a gun does not mean they may use it at any time. Good, they said. But wait, they wondered, why would someone want to carry a gun if they can't use it? Exactly, I thought: I don't see the logic either.

Rights in Historical Context

The second article in our nation's Bill of Rights preserves the individual's right to keep and bear arms. That may be the letter of the law, but even a minor history buff knows that in spirit, it was written primarily to reinforce citizens' right to organize a popular militia to protect homesteaders and communities from outside invasion. True, some states have long interpreted this amendment to incorporate the preservation of individuals' right to bear arms too. But I doubt if James Madison, the chief framer of the Bill of Rights, had the powerful, corporate gun industry lobby in mind as a prime force upholding "individuals'" rights.

Furthermore, if you read the Second Amendment in historical context, it speaks to a people still reeling from a violent political revolution, and, we must admit, an inverted kind of xenophobia. Many European colonists and westward moving settlers feared Native Americans, whose civil and human rights were quickly usurped in the name of the very freedom the revolutionaries claimed for themselves.

I suppose I ought to resist my urge to, let's say, target the phallocentric symbolism of the gun. Besides, the gun lobby has already beaten me to it. By local press accounts, it was NRA influence that pushed a recent "conceal carry" bill through the Minnesota legislature—coauthored by two nice ladies in suits and pearls, Rep. Linda Boudreau and Sen. Pat Pariseau. This new legislation was signed straightaway by our new, conservative young governor. Now, it's easier for Minnesota gun owners to obtain permits to carry their weapons on their person in public. A gun owner requesting a permit must be issued one provided he or she receives basic training in how to use the gun and passes the background check. By putting a feminine face on this bill, its handlers effectively subverted the perception that gun advocates are testosterone-laden bullies, shady pawnshop hangers-on or wacko separatists. An illusion is an illusion is an illusion.

So now the woman in line behind me in the supermarket might be packing. OK, maybe she's experienced the horror of rape and fears another attack. The guy sitting next to me at the Vikings [football] game in the Metrodome could have a pistol in his pocket. He might live out in the ex-urbs and have the perception that walking the dreaded city streets from the parking lot to the stadium is rife with danger. My neighbor down the street who shoots crows with his BB gun might switch to a .357. Let's hope he doesn't transfer his disaffection for the early-cawing birds to the late-night partying neighbors.

These folks might feel safer by being able to legally carry their firearms. I sure don't.

12

Gun-Free Zone Laws Prevent Gun Crime at Schools

Brady Center to Prevent Gun Violence

The Brady Center to Prevent Gun Violence is a grassroots organization that lobbies to enact and enforce laws designed to reduce gun violence. The center also works to educate the public about gun violence. The Brady Center was founded in the wake of the 1981 shooting of White House press secretary James Brady during an assassination attempt on President Ronald Reagan.

Policies that keep schools and campuses gun-free are one of the primary reasons that children are safer in school than in the world outside. However, if the gun lobby persuades states to overturn long-standing policies that allow schools and colleges to prohibit the possession of guns, schools will no longer be safe. Guns increase the risk of violence in schools and colleges. Moreover, violent acts and suicide attempts are more likely to be fatal when a gun is used. The only way to reduce the risk of gun violence in American schools is to keep them gun-free.

Despite the horrific massacre at Virginia Tech [on April 16, 2007], college and university campuses are much safer than the communities that surround them. A U.S. Justice Department study found that from 1995 to 2002, college students aged 18 to 24 experienced violence at significantly lower average annual rates—almost 20% lower—than non-students in the same age group. Moreover, 93% *of the violence against students occurs off campus.* Even 85% of the violent crimes against students who live on campus occur at locations off campus.

Elementary and secondary schools are also safer than society at large, as fewer than 1% of school-age homicide victims are killed on or around school grounds or on the way to and from school. Plus, in every year from 1992 to 2000, youths aged 5–19 were at least 70 times more likely to be murdered away from school than at a school. Even Gary Kleck, a researcher often cited by the gun lobby, notes these statistics and concludes: *"Both gun carrying and gun violence are thus phenomena almost entirely confined to the world outside schools."*

The discrepancy in violence rates on and off school grounds and on and off college campuses is no doubt due, in part, to the fact that nearly every academic institution—from elementary school through higher education—has adopted a policy that either tightly controls possession and use of student firearms or bans guns altogether. The overwhelming preference among Americans—94% according to one survey—is to keep it that way.

If . . . colleges and schools [are prohibited] from barring or controlling gun possession and use by their students, it is not difficult to imagine the increased dangers . . . that will follow.

Upsetting Long-Standing Policies

If the gun lobby is successful in getting state legislatures . . . to upset these long-standing policies and prohibit colleges and schools from barring or controlling gun possession and use by their students, it is not difficult to imagine the increased dangers and risks that will follow. They would, at a minimum, include:

- Diminished safety for students, faculty, staff, and visitors;

- Greater potential for student-on-student and student-on-faculty violence, and more lethal results when such violence occurs;

- An increased risk of suicide attempts ending in fatalities;

- An exponential increase in opportunities for gun theft and subsequent harm to people on and off campus; and

- Potentially huge legal, financial, and public-relations costs should gun violence occur as a result of these policies.

Schools have a legal duty to provide safe environments for their students, employees, and visitors. Courts have established that schools can be held liable if they do not take adequate measures to maintain a safe environment. Schools should have the authority to decide how to fulfill their legal duty to provide a safe environment without being undercut by the gun lobby's campaign to take away schools' discretion over this crucial safety issue. This duty will be undermined if the gun lobby's campaign is successful. Moreover, introducing guns on campus and into schools raises a host of public and student-relation problems.

Guns Increase School Violence

The primary threat posed by the gun lobby's campaign is to colleges and universities where students are old enough to be legally entitled to purchase or possess all manner of firearms. As everyone that has lived through adolescence and young-adulthood knows, the college age years—18 to 24—are among the most volatile periods in a person's life. The Bureau of Alcohol, Tobacco, Firearms and Explosives (ATF) has consistently found that criminal gun possession is highest for youths 18 to 24, with the ages 19–21 providing an even higher peak within this range. These also happen to be the peak years for persons to commit violent gun crimes, including homicides.

To arm all students may well make it easier for those bent on carrying out destruction to bring guns onto campus.

Also, no one should forget that [Virginia Tech shooter] *Seung Hui Cho was a 23-year-old student who the Commonwealth of Virginia thought was a lawful firearms purchaser.* Moreover, having missed the fact that he had been adjudicated mentally defective in December 2005, Virginia would have issued a CCW [carrying concealed weapons] license to Cho had he applied. How many other individuals that have carried out school shootings were legally entitled to purchase or possess firearms at the time of the shootings? We are not aware of anyone having made a count, though a review of . . . school shootings . . . indicates many of those shooters were so qualified. Thus, the policy solution advocated by the gun lobby to arm all students may well make it easier for those bent on carrying out destruction to bring guns onto campus.

There are a host of reasons why gun violence is likely to increase, perhaps dramatically, if students are able to keep and carry guns on college campuses. . . .

The Problem of Drugs and Alcohol

The prevalence of alcohol and drugs on college campuses is a prime reason to keep guns out. Binge drinking is highest among 18–24 year olds. Illegal drug use also peaks during these volatile years. Both activities are common among college students. For example, according to a new study by the National Center on Addiction and Substance Abuse at Columbia University, "[n]early half of America's 5.4 million full-time college students abuse drugs or drink alcohol on binges at least once a month." For college gun owners, the rate of binge drinking is even higher—two-thirds. Of course, both drug and alcohol use greatly increases the risks of injury to users and those around them. Alcohol, for example, "is involved in two thirds of college student suicides, in 90% of campus rapes, and in 95% of the violent crime on campus." Almost 700,000 students between the ages of 18 and 24 are assaulted each year by another student who has been drinking. If guns were involved, those assaults would be much more likely to be fatal. Guns, alcohol, and drugs have proven to be an extremely dangerous mix. Drinking alcohol can even make a police officer "unfit for duty." . . .

Colleges and universities have many programs in place to address drug and alcohol abuse, but it is unlikely that campus drug and alcohol problems will be eliminated any time soon. Therefore, it is even more critical that schools be able to ban or tightly control firearms possession and use by students. A binge-drinking, drug-using student is dangerous enough; let's not give him or her a gun.

Suicide and Mental Health Issues

Mental health issues and the risks of suicides among college students is another prime reason to prohibit or limit access to guns by college students. Researchers have found that youths aged 18–25 experience the highest rate of mental health problems. According to the American College Health Association's National College Health Assessment, between 9 and 11% of college students seriously considered suicide in the last school year. Even more alarming, every year about 1,100 college students commit suicide and another 24,000 attempt to do so.

Introducing firearms into this psychological cauldron could dramatically increase the danger to students. If a gun is used in a suicide attempt, more than 90% of the time the attempt will be fatal. By comparison, suicide attempts made by overdosing on drugs are fatal only 3% of the time. Thus, while suicides involving firearms account for only 5% of the suicide attempts in America, they accounted for more than half of the 32,439 fatalities. Needless to say, increasing firearms availability for college students could lead to a significant increase in the number of fatalities among the 24,000 suicide attempts survived by students each year. After all, the presence of a gun in the home increases the risk of suicide fivefold.

The only safe and non-discriminatory way to reduce the risks of gun violence on college campuses is to keep them gun-free.

Colleges and universities have devoted considerable resources to address mental health problems and suicide risks on campus. One thing they have not done, however, is attempt to expel all the students that pose mental health or suicide risks. Nor should they. A college may face legal problems if it discriminates against certain students based on a perception that they are prone to depression or violence. Moreover, many scholars believe it is not possible to reliably identify who will go on a rampage, thus suggesting there is no way for a college or university to distinguish in advance between guntoters who pose extraordinary risks, and those who may not. According to Dr. James Alan Fox, Dean of the College of Criminal Justice at Northeastern University and one of America's leading criminologists:

> It's not a matter of identifying problem cases and dealing with them. It's a matter of changing the way things are done. . . . You can't just grease the squeaky wheel. You've got to grease the whole machine.

Accordingly, the only safe and non-discriminatory way to reduce the risks of gun violence on college campuses is to keep them gun-free. . . .

Accidental Shootings

In addition to the risk factors above, allowing more guns on college campuses and into schools is likely to increase the risk of students being shot accidentally. Guns in the home are four times as likely to be used in unintentional shootings than in self-defense. Plus, a 1991 report by the General Accounting Office that surveyed unintentional firearm fatalities found that 23% of those deaths occurred because the person firing the gun was unaware whether the gun was loaded. The report explains several ways in which this happens. "For example, one might empty a firearm but not notice that a round remains in the chamber, one might typically leave a weapon unloaded and so assume that it is always unloaded, or one might pull the trigger several times without discharge (dry-firing) and so assume the chamber is empty even though it is not." These mistakes are not limited to children. Even trained gun users have made them.

If there are no guns on campus, these types of accidents cannot occur.

13

Gun-Free Zone Laws Increase Gun Crime at Schools

Ann Coulter

Ann Coulter is a conservative syndicated columnist and author of several books, including High Crimes and Misdemeanors *and* If Democrats Had Any Brains, They'd Be Republicans.

Gun-free school zone laws do not protect students from mass murderers. In fact, such policies make schools popular targets. There will always be violent, unbalanced people who turn to mass murder. The only policy known to deter their murderous rampages is to allow law-abiding citizens to carry concealed weapons. Indeed, studies show that concealed weapons reduce the death toll in multiple-shooting incidents. Students, faculty, and staff will be safer if those who have a permit to carry a concealed weapon are not banned from carrying their weapons on school grounds.

From the [terrorist] attacks of 9/11 [2001] to [the Virginia Tech] school shooting [on April 16, 2007], after every mass murder there is an overwhelming urge to "do something" to prevent a similar attack.

But since Adam ate the apple and let evil into the world, deranged individuals have existed.

Most of the time they can't be locked up until it's too late. It's not against the law to be crazy—in some jurisdictions it actually makes you more viable as a candidate for public office.

It's certainly not against the law to be an unsociable loner. If it were, [consumer advocate] Ralph Nader would be behind bars right now, where he belongs. Mass murder is often the first serious crime unbalanced individuals are caught committing—as appears to be the case of the Virginia Tech shooter.

The best we can do is enact policies that will reduce the death toll when these acts of carnage occur, as they will in a free and open society of 300 million people, most of whom have cable TV.

Deterring Mass Murder

Only one policy has ever been shown to deter mass murder: concealed-carry laws. In a comprehensive study of all public, multiple-shooting incidents in America between 1977 and 1999, the inestimable economists John Lott and Bill Landes found that concealed-carry laws were the only laws that had any beneficial effect.

And the effect was not insignificant. States that allowed citizens to carry concealed handguns reduced multiple-shooting attacks by 60 percent and reduced the death and injury from these attacks by nearly 80 percent.

The reason schools are consistently popular targets for mass murderers is precisely because of all the idiotic 'Gun-Free School Zone' laws.

Apparently, even crazy people prefer targets that can't shoot back. The reason schools are consistently popular targets for mass murderers is precisely because of all the idiotic "Gun-Free School Zone" laws.

From the people who brought you "zero tolerance," I present the Gun-Free Zone! Yippee! Problem solved! *Bam! Bam! Everybody down! Hey, how did that deranged loner get a gun into this Gun-Free Zone?*

It isn't the angst of adolescence. Plenty of school shootings have been committed by adults with absolutely no reason to be at the school, such as Laurie Dann, who shot up the Hubbard Woods Elementary School in Winnetka, Ill., in 1988; Patrick Purdy, who opened fire on children at Cleveland Elementary School in Stockton, Calif., in 1989; and Charles Carl Roberts, who murdered five schoolgirls at an Amish school in Lancaster County, Pa. [in 2006].

Oh by the way, the other major "Gun-Free Zone" in America is the post office.

But instantly, on the day of the shooting at Virginia Tech, the media were already promoting gun control and preemptively denouncing right-wingers who point out that gun control enables murderers rather than stopping them. Liberals get to lobby for gun control, but we're [i.e., conservatives] disallowed from arguing back. That's how good their arguments are. They're *that* good.

Needless to say, Virginia Tech is a Gun-Free School Zone—at least until [April 16, 2007]. The gunman must not have known. Imagine his embarrassment! Perhaps there should be signs.

Disarming Students

Virginia Tech even prohibits students with concealed-carry permits from carrying their guns on campus. [In 2006], the school disciplined a student for carrying a gun on campus, despite his lawful concealed-carry permit. If only someone like that had been in Norris Hall on [April 16, 2007], this massacre could have been ended a lot sooner.

But [in January 2007], the Virginia General Assembly shot down a bill that would have prevented universities like Virginia Tech from giving sanctuary to mass murderers on college campuses in Virginia by disarming students with concealed-carry permits valid in the rest of the state.

Virginia Tech spokesman Larry Hincker praised the legislature for allowing the school to disarm lawful gun owners on the faculty and student body, thereby surrendering every college campus in the state to deranged mass murderers, saying: "I'm sure the university community is appreciative of the General Assembly's actions because this will help parents, students, faculty and visitors feel safe on our campus."

Others disagreed. Writing [in 2006] about another dangerous killer who had been loose on the Virginia Tech campus, graduate student Jonathan McGlumphy wrote: "Is it not obvious that all students, faculty and staff would have been safer if (concealed handgun permit) holders were not banned from carrying their weapons on campus?"

If it wasn't obvious then, it is now.

14

Bans on Assault Weapons Increase Public Safety

Nicholas D. Kristof

Nicholas D. Kristof, a two-time Pulitzer Prize winner, writes op-ed columns for the New York Times.

Assault weapons pose a serious threat to public safety and should be banned. While only a small number of Americans owned assault weapons before they were banned, these weapons were involved in a disproportionate share of the nation's gun crimes. Even after the ban, assault weapons were used in one of five fatal police-officer shootings. Refusing to ban assault weapons will only lead to the deaths of more Americans.

If you've been longing for your very own assault rifle and 30-round magazine for the next holiday season, you're in luck.

President [George W.] Bush, sidestepping a promise, is allowing the ban on assault rifles and oversized clips to expire on Sept. 14 [2004]. So at a gun store here in Meridian [Idaho], a bit west of Boise, the counter has a display promising "2 FREE HIGH-CAPACITY MAGAZINES."

All you have to do is purchase a new Beretta 9-millimeter handgun and you'll receive two high-capacity magazines—on the condition, the fine print states, that the federal ban expires on schedule.

President Bush promised in the [2000] presidential campaign to support an extension of the ban, which was put in place in 1994 for 10 years. "It makes no sense for assault weapons to be around our society," Mr. Bush observed at the time.

These days Mr. Bush still says that he'll sign an extension of the ban if it happens to reach his desk. But he knows that the only way the ban can be extended on time is if he actually urges its passage, and he refuses to do that. So his promise to support an extension rings hollow—it's not exactly a lie, but it's not the full truth, either.

Mr. Bush's flip-flop is surprising because he has generally had the courage of his convictions. Apparently he's hiding from this issue because it's so politically charged.

Frustrating Loopholes

Critics of the assault weapon ban have one valid point: the ban has more holes than Swiss cheese.

"The big frustration of my customers is that [the ban] removed things that were kind of fun and made it look cool, but didn't affect how the gun operated," said Sean Wontor, a salesman who heaved two rifles onto the counter of Sportsman's Warehouse here in Meridian to make his point.

Assault weapons . . . account for a hugely disproportionate share of gun violence.

One was an assault weapon that was produced before the ban (and thus still legal), and the other was a sanitized version produced afterward to comply with the ban by removing the bayonet mount and the flash suppressor.

After these cosmetic changes, the rifle is now no longer considered an assault weapon, yet, of course, it is just as lethal.

Still, assault weapons, while amounting to only 1 percent of America's 190 million privately owned guns, account for a hugely disproportionate share of gun violence precisely because of their macho appeal.

Assault weapons aren't necessary for any kind of hunting or target shooting, but they're popular because they can transform a suburban [meek and mild-mannered] Walter Mitty [type man] into [a vengeful] Rambo, for a lot less money than a Hummer.

"I've got a ton of customers shooting squirrels with AK-47's," said Kevin Tester, a gun salesman near Boise. "They're using 30-round magazines and 7.62-millimeter ammunition, they're shooting up the hills, and they're having a blast."

I grew up on an Oregon farm that bristled with guns to deal with the coyotes that dined on our sheep. Having fired everything from a pistol to a machine gun, I can testify that shooting can be a lot of fun. But consider the cost: 29,000 gun deaths in America each year.

[Assault weapons] are still used in one in five fatal shootings of police officers.

A Special Problem

While gun statistics are as malleable as Play-Doh, they do underscore that assault weapons are a special problem in America.

They accounted for 8.4 percent of the guns traced to crimes between 1988 and 1991, and they are still used in one in five fatal shootings of police officers. If anything, we should be plugging the holes in the ban by having it cover copycat weapons without bayonet mounts, instead of moving backward and allowing a new flood of weapons and high-capacity magazines.

The bottom line is that Mr. Bush's waffling on assault weapons will mean more dead Americans.

About 100 times as many Americans are already dying from gunfire in the U.S. as in Iraq. As many Americans die from firearms every six weeks as died in the 9/11 [2001, terrorist] attacks—yet the White House is paralyzed on this issue.

Mr. Bush needs to live up to his campaign promise and push to keep the ban on assault weapons. [The ban expired in September 2004.] Otherwise, we'll bring more of the Iraq-like carnage to our own shores, and his refusal to confront our gun problem will kill more Americans over time than [9/11 mastermind] Osama bin Laden ever could.

15

Bans on Assault Weapons Will Not Reduce Crime

Robert J. Caldwell

Robert J. Caldwell is former editor of the San Diego Union-Tribune's *Insight section.*

Banning assault weapons in 1994 did not reduce gun crime. In fact, studies show that criminals use pistols, not semiautomatic rifles, when committing crimes. What drove the federal ban on assault weapons was the gun's threatening appearance, not any actual danger posed. Indeed, even before the federal ban, criminals rarely used assault weapons in their crimes. Law-abiding citizens should not be prevented from owning weapons that do not threaten public safety.

[Former] House Majority Leader Tom DeLay (R.-Tex.), the tough conservative liberals love to hate, provoked a mini-furor not long ago by declaring that the Republican-controlled House would not renew Congress' 1994 ban on so-called assault weapons. Only reflexive gun banners and the uninformed can have been disconcerted. The 1994 ban proved predictably ineffective. Letting it expire on schedule in 2004 would change, well, almost nothing. The ban, championed by California's formidable Sen. Dianne Feinstein, (D.) was sold on a singularly false, if well-intentioned, premise—that the semi-automatic (one shot for each trigger pull), civilian versions of certain military-type rifles were major contributors to crime. These firearms, we were typically told by ban advocates, were the "guns of choice for gang bangers, drug dealers and street criminals." Wrong, wrong, wrong.

Assault Weapons Rarely Used in Gun Crimes

In fact, the truth was exactly opposite. The U.S. Department of Justice, the U.S. Bureau of Alcohol, Tobacco and Firearms [BATF], the FBI, the law enforcement statistics of every state bothering to count and the careful research of criminologists all told the same story: Rifles of any type are used in only a tiny fraction of gun crimes—the preferred firearm for nearly all criminals being the easily concealed handgun. The criminal use of rifles dubbed assault weapons is rarer still. Indeed, so-called assault rifles are the least likely firearms to be used in crime.

[Police] officers 'are more likely to confront an escaped tiger from the local zoo than to confront an assault rifle in the hands of a drug-crazed killer on the streets.'

FBI statistics show that rifles of any description are used in only about 3% of homicides each year. Data compiled by criminologist Gary Kleck put the frequency of assault weapons use in all violent crime at 0.5%.

In California, a statewide survey of law enforcement agencies by the state Department of Justice found that a mere 3.7% of firearms used in homicides and assaults were assault weapons. A Trenton, N.J., deputy police chief said his officers "are more likely to confront an escaped tiger from the local zoo than to confront an assault rifle in the hands of a drug-crazed killer on the streets."

No wonder, then, that banning this arbitrarily defined class of firearms had no discernible effect on crime.

Studies Show Weapon Ban Ineffective

The U.S. Department of Justice conducted two studies of the consequences of the 1994 assault weapons ban. In 1999, [President] Bill Clinton's Justice Department looked exhaustively at the ban's effects. It concluded that "the public safety benefits of the 1994 ban have not yet been demonstrated." In 2001, a second Justice Department review similarly found no evidence that the ban had a statistically significant effect on violent crime. A congressionally mandated study by the Urban Institute reached comparable conclusions.

Banning Feinstein's 19 types of semi-automatic rifles and pistols because they have two or more military-style features—such as a bayonet lug, pistol grip or flash suppressor—is irrelevant to crime. When was the last drive-by bayoneting?

The Feinstein ban's prohibition on newly manufactured ammunition magazines capable of containing more than 10 rounds, for rifles or handguns, might seem a prudent public-safety precaution. But, again, there is no conclusive evidence over nearly a decade that smaller-capacity magazines have any crime-reduction or violence-reduction effects.

But isn't there something to be said for the gun banners' chronic plea that any restrictions reducing the numbers of guns Americans own makes society safer?

In a word, no.

If the simplistic notion that more guns equal more crime and more homicides had any validity, crime rates would have climbed during the decade.

More Firearms Do Not Equal More Crime

The 200 million-plus privately owned firearms in the United States grew by an estimated 37 million during the 1990s. If the simplistic notion that more guns equal more crime and more homicides had any validity, crime rates would have climbed during the decade. Instead, rates for serious and violent crime fell every year from 1991 through the end of the decade. Despite those 37 million more guns, murder rates in many major American cities fell to the lowest levels in 40 years.

Thirty-five states have enacted "right-to-carry" legislation allowing law-abiding citizens a license to carry a concealed weapon. In most if not all of these 35 states, homicide rates declined after ordinary citizens were permitted the means of self-defense.

Most of the 19 rifle and pistol types banned by Feinstein's 1994 amendment were already barred from import into the United States by order of the Bureau of Alcohol, Tobacco and Firearms in 1989. Even if Feinstein's ban expires, the BATF's import restrictions would still be in place. The two domestic manufacturers of assault-style pistols are out of business. That leaves a possible resumption in production of one domestically produced rifle, the Colt AR-15, on Feinstein's list as the sole likely consequence of the 1994 ban's expiration. Feinstein's magazine-capacity restrictions would lapse with the ban's expiration. But they are widely circumvented now anyway by the vast numbers of pre-ban magazines legally available.

Ban Has Weak Political Support

The gun banners also miscalculate the political support for more restrictions that limit the firearm-owning rights of law-abiding citizens.

Feinstein would expand her ban if she could but she cannot get 51 votes in the Senate. Rep. Carolyn McCarthy, a New York Democrat, proposes banning millions more semi-automatic rifles and pistols owned and used by American hunters, sport shooters and collectors. Her bill stands no chance.

A White House aide says President [George W.] Bush favors extending the Feinstein ban, a position he took with no visible conviction during the 2000 campaign. Bush himself says nothing now, no doubt because he knows the gun-rights vote in swing states Arkansas, Tennessee and West Virginia made him president.

DeLay predicts the House won't vote to make the 1994 ban permanent. He's probably right, and that's no loss to the country. [The ban expired in September 2004.]

16

People Have the Right to Defend Themselves with Guns

Alan Contreras

Alan Contreras is administrator of the Office of Degree Authorization of the Oregon Student Assistance Commission.

People should be able to use guns to defend themselves. In isolated rural areas, for example, people need to protect themselves from dangerous wildlife. Moreover, there are often fewer police officers in isolated communities. Even in cities, the police cannot be everywhere at once. Reasonable bans on certain weapons such as machine guns or restrictions on carrying concealed weapons into the courtroom are necessary. However, broad bans that prohibit private, law-abiding citizens from carrying weapons are unreasonable.

The [April 16, 2007,] shootings at Virginia Tech have raised an old question: Should we allow responsible people to own guns to protect themselves and others?

In Defense of Self-Defense

Along with about 7,000 of the 325,000 people in my county, I have a permit from the sheriff to carry a concealed gun. Many more people keep guns in their homes, for which a permit is not required. In fact, no permit is required to carry a gun openly in my state of Oregon, or in most other states, although that practice is so uncommon outside very rural areas that most people don't realize it is legal.

Some of the people at the colleges and universities I visit as part of my job probably didn't know that I carry a gun on their campuses. Now they do. I carry it as protection from criminal attacks; and I couldn't have gotten a permit if I had a serious criminal record or had been hospitalized for psychiatric problems.

Surely each person has the right to decide whether to kill or die.

I know how to operate my gun safely; I know when I can use it legally; and I never leave it where anybody else could take it. I practice shooting at a range, to make sure that I remain competent. Yet even some of my friends think I am strange, possibly wicked, for owning a gun. I don't understand that view. Surely each person has the right to decide whether to kill or die—and that is the choice we are talking about.

Should I—a 51-year-old bookworm with no significant biceps—have to defend myself with a broom handle if a knife-wielding thug attacks me in my yard? It is true that, given reasonable warning, I might be able to run away. But why make me run off my property merely because some criminal has run onto it? Though I was raised a Quaker, I no longer accept that flight is morally superior to self-defense.

The Decision to Carry a Gun

One reason for my decision to carry a gun is that I live in a small city in the mostly rural Western United States. In rural areas, guns are readily available to criminals and unwilling victims alike.

Also common in the West are some of the less congenial animals. Cougars have entered the city where I live twice in recent years; one hid under a house. Black bears are common, although they are usually not dangerous. Usually. Wolverines live at one place where I go birding every year, and where many people camp. I once went to a small store in southeastern Oregon and found a rattlesnake guarding the doorway. Granted, snakes can usually be escorted away with a long-handled push broom (after being swept away from the store, the serpent promptly slithered under the driver's side of my car, where it waited in the shade), but I don't always carry a broom.

Of course, the key issue in most people's minds is whether, in an emergency, it is right to use a gun not against an animal, but against a human. Some people would not shoot another person in self-defense. I would.

The argument that the police can't be everywhere may sound like a cliché from the National Rifle Association, of which I am not a member—not believing in a personal right to own machine guns or armor-piercing bullets. In fact, it is an important reality. There are few police officers in rural America; those we do have (my father was one) are usually located in isolated towns. In some parts of Oregon where I go, the nearest police officer may be 50 miles away, across uninhabited country.

That fact adds to the general libertarian attitude in the West of preferring to solve problems personally. Sometimes government help is not an option: The district attorney of my county announced several years ago that no misdemeanors and only major property crimes would be prosecuted, owing to a lack of resources. In effect, he transferred the economic burden of resolving "minor" crimes from the public coffers to citizens' insurance rates.

There is certainly something macabre about the idea, shown graphically in a cartoon shortly after the Virginia Tech shootings [of April 16, 2007], that we should just let the good guys and bad guys shoot it out. Yet it is even worse to pretend that the good guys and bad guys should be treated as morally equivalent.

The question of who should be allowed to own a gun is a legitimate one, and it is proper to ban private guns from certain places, like courtrooms. But let's argue about gun ownership from a coherent moral and factual position, not from the gut reactions of any one moment, however tragic that moment may be.

17

Freedom Does Not Include Unrestricted Access to Guns

Philadelphia Inquirer

The Philadelphia Inquirer *is a daily newspaper that serves the Philadelphia, Pennsylvania, area.*

Freedom does not mean that people may exercise their rights at the expense of others. Indeed, true freedom comes with responsibility. While the U.S. Constitution grants people the right to bear arms, people may not exercise this right at the expense of other people's right to "life, liberty and the pursuit of happiness." Allowing students the unfettered right to carry guns will not make students safer. In fact, it was a sick sense of individualism and the unfettered access to guns that allowed Cho Seung-Hui to kill thirty-two people plus himself on the campus of Virginia Tech on April 16, 2007.

> "We create the world in which we live; if that world becomes unfit for human life, it is because we tire of our responsibility."

British author Cyril Connolly wrote those words in 1938. The [April 16, 2007, shooting at Virginia Tech] ... gives them fresh relevance—and offers a starting point for a national conversation on the role of responsibility in a society that prizes liberty and individualism. Cho Seung-Hui, 23, exploited those aspects of the American character to kill 32 others and himself ... at Virginia Tech. Liberty and individualism have produced great inventors, inspiring artists, brilliant thinkers. They also create space for evil acts. Using the liberty that America and Virginia afforded him, Cho bought two handguns and ammunition despite a history of mental-health problems and threatening gestures toward others. Acting on a sick individualism, he took those guns and made sad history. As the funerals begin, Americans ask, why does this keep happening to us? Let no one misunderstand: Cho is responsible for killing those 32 people. But his rampage raises broader issues that begin to explain why this keeps happening to us. One issue is how the country's advocacy groups shape—make that, misshape—issues and solutions. The gun lobby has framed the gun violence debate perversely to its advantage—and done a powerful job of it. It is time for adults to stand up and demand that reality prevail.

The most extreme gun rights advocates seized upon the [Virginia Tech] shootings and declared that they could have been averted if only Virginia law did not ban guns on college campuses. The core problem, according to the gun lobby, is that Americans do not have enough access to firearms.

The right to bear arms should not be allowed to overpower others' right to 'life, liberty and the pursuit of happiness.'

The gun lobby is fond of demanding that those who seek mere limits on gun ownership guarantee ahead of time that those limits will work perfectly and solve the problem fully. OK, let's turn it around. Please explain how putting more firepower within easy reach of adolescents, with their penchants for depression, romantic drama, and binge drinking, would make campuses safer. Let's keep turning the tables. Instead of forcing anti-violence activists to prove a point most don't believe—that gun control is the sole solution—let's force the National Rifle Association to explain why gun violence is so much lower in other Western industrialized societies. If it's not their far stricter gun control, what is it? Are they better people than we are? Dramatic rampages like [the shooting at Virginia Tech] just don't happen in other nations with the frequency they do here. Few European cities experience anything like the steady drip of deadly shootings that Philadelphia does. And when guns spill innocent blood abroad, that often spurs efforts to keep guns out of the hands of the criminal and the mentally ill, such as Cho. Australian Prime Minister John Howard has been a strong ally of President [George W.] Bush's war in Iraq. But he is on the other side of the world when it comes to gun regulations. When a shooter killed 35 people in Australia in 1996, action was taken to limit the availability of guns, which has led to significantly fewer shooting deaths. "We showed a national resolve that the gun culture that is such a negative in the United States would never become a negative in our country," Howard said. . . . America is defining deviancy down. That tendency will continue if tighter gun restrictions do not flow from the killings. To be a free society does not require enabling the unfettered exercise of dangerous behavior. Every right in the Constitution comes with responsibilities. A free press still may not defame with impunity. Religious freedom does not empower adults to harm children. And rights do come into conflict. That's why we have a Supreme Court. The right to bear arms should not be allowed to overpower others' right to "life, liberty and the pursuit of happiness." Lawmakers, especially the cowardly Democrats now in charge of the House of Representatives and Senate, have the responsibility to treat violence as a dire public health issue rather than an electoral albatross. They need to look at reality (isn't that what Democrats have criticized President Bush for ignoring in Iraq?) and stand up against the powerful gun lobby to enact tighter gun regulations. Voters, if they feel strongly enough about changing the culture of violence, should reject elected officials who avoid that responsibility. "We create the world in which we live; if that world becomes unfit for human life, it is because we tire of our responsibility." For too many years, those who shudder at tragedies like [the one at Virginia Tech] . . . have shirked their responsibility to create a world that is fit and safe for our children. If we do not rouse ourselves from our languor, the percussion of gun violence will quicken.

Organizations to Contact

The editors have compiled the following list of organizations concerned with the issues debated in this book. The descriptions are derived from materials provided by the organizations. All have publications or information available for interested readers. The list was compiled on the date of publication of the present volume; the information provided here may change. Be aware that many organizations may take several weeks or longer to respond to inquiries, so allow as much time as possible.

American Civil Liberties Union (ACLU)
125 Broad St., 18th Fl., New York, NY   10004-2400
(212) 549-2500
e-mail: aclu@aclu.org
Web site: www.aclu.org

The ACLU champions the rights set forth in the U.S. Constitution and the Bill of Rights. The union interprets the Second Amendment as a guarantee to form militias, not as a guarantee of the individual right to own and bear firearms and believes that gun control is constitutional and necessary. The ACLU publishes the semiannual *Civil Liberties* in addition to policy statements and reports, many of which are available on its Web site.

Brady Campaign to Prevent Gun Violence/Brady Center to Prevent Gun Violence
1225 Eye St. NW, Ste. 1100, Washington, DC   20005
Campaign: (202) 898-0792; Center: (202) 289-7319
• fax: Campaign: (202) 371-9615; Center: (202) 408-1851
Web sites: www.bradycampaign.org; www.bradycenter.org

Established by former White House press secretary and gun violence victim James Brady and his wife, Sarah, the Brady Campaign and the Brady Center's primary goal is to create an America free from gun violence. Through grassroots activism both organizations work to reform the gun industry, educate the public about gun violence, and develop sensible regulations to reduce gun violence. The organizations publish facts sheets, issue briefs, and special reports on their Web sites, including "Kids and Guns in America" and "Domestic Violence and Guns."

Cato Institute
1000 Massachusetts Ave. NW, Washington, DC   20001
(202) 842-0200 • fax: (202) 842-3490
e-mail: librarian@cato.org
Web site: www.cato.org

The Cato Institute is a libertarian public-policy research foundation. It evaluates government policies and offers reform proposals and commentary on its Web site. Its publications include articles such as "Fighting Back: Crime, Self-Defense, and the Right to Carry a Handgun" and "Trust the People: The Case Against Gun Control." It also publishes the magazine *Regulation*, the *Cato Policy Report*, and books such as *The Samurai, the Mountie, and the Cowboy: Should America Adopt the Gun Controls of Other Democracies?*

Citizens Committee for the Right to Keep and Bear Arms
12500 NE Tenth Pl., Bellevue, WA   98005
(425) 454-4911 • fax: (425) 451-3959
e-mail: informationrequest@ccrkba.org
Web site: www.ccrkba.org

The committee believes that the U.S. Constitution's Second Amendment guarantees and protects the right of individual Americans to own guns. The organization works to educate the public concerning this right and to lobby legislators to prevent the passage of gun-control laws. The committee is affiliated with the Second Amendment Foundation and has more than six hundred thousand members. It publishes several magazines, including *Gun Week*, *Women & Guns*, and *Gun News Digest*. News releases, fact sheets, and editorials from its publications are available on its Web site.

Coalition for Gun Control

1488 Queen St. West, Toronto, ON   M6K 3K3
(416) 604-0209 • fax: (416) 604-0209
e-mail: 71417.763@compuserve.com
Web site: www.guncontrol.ca

The coalition was founded in the wake of the Montreal massacre in which a man with a Ruger Mini-14 and large-capacity
magazine shot twenty-eight people at l'École Polytechnique,
killing fourteen young female engineering students. The Canadian organization was formed to reduce gun death, injury,
and crime. It supports strict safe gun storage requirements,
possession permits, a complete ban on assault weapons, and
tougher restrictions on handguns. The coalition publishes
press releases and backgrounders. Its Web site provides information on firearms deaths and injuries, illegal gun trafficking,
and Canada's gun-control law.

Coalition to Stop Gun Violence (CSGV)

1023 Fifteenth St. NW, Ste. 301, Washington, DC   20005
(202) 408-0061
Web site: www.csgv.org

The CSGV lobbies at the local, state, and federal levels to ban
the sale of handguns to individuals and to institute licensing
and registration of all firearms. It also litigates cases against
firearms makers. Its publications include various informa-
tional sheets on gun violence and the *Annual Citizens' Conference to Stop Gun Violence Briefing Book*, a compendium of
gun-control fact sheets, arguments, and resources. On its Web
site, CSGV publishes articles on assault weapons, gun laws,
and other gun-violence issues.

Gun Owners of America (GOA)

8001 Forbes Pl., Ste. 102, Springfield, VA   22151
(703) 321-8585 • fax: (703) 321-8408
e-mail: goamail@gunoweners.org
Web site: www.gunowners.org

GOA is a nonprofit lobbying organization that defends the Second Amendment rights of gun owners. It has developed a network of attorneys to help fight court battles to protect gun owners' rights. GOA also works with members of Congress, state legislators, and local citizens to protect gun ranges and local gun clubs from closure by the government. On its Web site the organization publishes fact sheets and links to op-ed articles, including "People Don't Stop Killers, People with Guns Do" and "Is Arming Teachers the Solution to School Shootings?"

Independence Institute
13952 Denver West Pkwy., Ste. 400, Golden, CO   80401
(303) 279-6536 • fax: (303) 279-4176
e-mail: amy@i2i.org
Web site: www.i2i.org

The institute is a pro–free market think tank that supports gun ownership as both a civil liberty and a constitutional right. Its Web site contains articles, fact sheets, and commentary from a variety of sources and includes "Making Schools Safe for Criminals," "Is Gun Control a New Religion?" and "Kids and Guns: The Politics of Panic."

Jews for the Preservation of Firearms Ownership (JPFO)
PO Box 270143, Hartford, WI   53027
(262) 673-9745 • fax: (262) 673-9746
e-mail: jpfo@jpfo.org
Web site: www.jpfo.org

JPFO is an educational organization that believes Jewish law mandates self-defense. Its primary goal is the elimination of the idea that gun control is a socially useful public policy in any country. On its Web site JPFO provides links to firearms commentary.

National Crime Prevention Council (NCPC)
2345 Crystal Dr., 5th Fl., Arlington, VA   22202-4801

(202) 466-6272 • fax: (202) 296-1356
Web site: www.ncpc.org

The NCPC is a branch of the U.S. Department of Justice. Through its programs and educational materials, the council works to teach Americans how to reduce crime and to address its causes. It provides readers with information on gun control and gun violence. The NCPC's publications include the newsletter *Catalyst*, which is published ten times a year, and articles, brochures, and fact sheets, many of which are available on its Web site.

National Rifle Association of America (NRA)
11250 Waples Mill Rd., Fairfax, VA   22030
(703) 267-1000 • fax: (703) 267-3989
Web site: www.nra.org

With nearly three million members, the NRA is America's largest organization of gun owners. It is also the primary lobbying group for those who oppose gun-control laws. The NRA believes that such laws violate the U.S. Constitution and do nothing to reduce crime. In addition to its monthly magazines *America's 1st Freedom*, *American Rifleman*, *American Hunter*, *InSights*, and *Shooting Sports USA*, the NRA publishes numerous books, bibliographies, reports, and pamphlets on gun ownership, gun safety, and gun control, some of which are available on its Web site.

Second Amendment Foundation
12500 NE Tenth Pl., Bellevue, WA   98005
(206) 454-7012 • fax: (206) 451-3959
Web site: www.saf.org

A sister organization to the Citizens Committee for the Right to Keep and Bear Arms, the foundation is dedicated to informing Americans about their Second Amendment right to keep and bear firearms. It believes that gun-control laws violate this right. The foundation publishes numerous books, including *Armed: New Perspectives on Gun Control, CCW: Carry-*

ing Concealed Weapons, and *The Concealed Handgun Manual: How to Choose, Carry, and Shoot a Gun in Self Defense.* Reports, articles, and commentary on gun issues are available on its Web site.

U.S. Department of Justice(DOJ) Office of Justice Programs

810 Seventh St. NW, Washington, DC   20531
Phone and e-mail for specific bureaus and offices are available at www.ojp.usdoj.gov/contactus.htm
Web site: www.ojp.usdoj.gov

The Department of Justice strives to protect citizens by maintaining effective law enforcement, crime prevention, crime detection, and prosecution and rehabilitation of offenders. Through its Office of Justice Programs, the department operates the National Institute of Justice, the Office of Juvenile Justice and Delinquency Prevention, and the Bureau of Justice Statistics. The Bureau of Justice Statistics provides research on crime and criminal justice. The offices of the DOJ publish a variety of crime-related documents on their respective Web sites.

Violence Policy Center

1730 Rhode Island Ave. NW, Ste. 1014
Washington, DC   20036
(202) 822-8200 • fax: (202) 822-8205
Web site: www.vpc.org

The center is an educational foundation that conducts research on firearms violence. It works to educate the public concerning the dangers of guns and supports gun-control measures. The center's publications include *Drive-By America, A Shrinking Minority: The Continuing Decline of Gun Ownership in America,* and *When Men Murder Women: An Analysis of 2005 Homicide Data.* On the center's Web site are fact sheets, press releases, and studies on concealed-carry laws, assault weapons, and other firearm violence issues.

Bibliography

Books

Amnesty International — *The Impact of Guns on Women's Lives.* Oxford, UK: Oxfam International, 2005.

Ian Ayres and John J. Donohue — *Shooting Down the More Guns, Less Crime Hypothesis.* Cambridge, MA: National Bureau of Economic Research, 2002.

Arnold Grossman — *One Nation Under Guns: An Essay on an American Epidemic.* Golden, CO: Fulcrum, 2006.

Bernard E. Harcourt — *Language of the Gun: Youth, Crime, and Public Policy.* Chicago: University of Chicago Press, 2006.

Darnell F. Hawkins, ed. — *Violent Crime: Assessing Race and Ethnic Differences.* New York: Cambridge University Press, 2003.

David Hemenway — *Private Guns, Public Health.* Ann Arbor: University of Michigan Press, 2004.

James B. Jacobs — *Can Gun Control Work?* New York: Oxford University Press, 2002.

Wayne R. LaPierre — *Guns, Freedom and Terrorism.* Nashville, TN: WND Books, 2003.

John R. Lott — *The Bias Against Guns: Why Almost Everything You've Heard About Gun Control Is Wrong.* Washington, DC: Regnery, 2003.

H. Naci Mocan and Erdal Teken — *Guns, Drugs and Juvenile Crime: Evidence from a Panel of Siblings and Twins.* Cambridge, MA: National Bureau of Economic Research, 2003.

Robert J. Spitzer — *The Politics of Gun Control.* Washington, DC: CQ Press, 2008.

Irvin Waller — *Less Law, More Order: The Truth About Reducing Crime.* Westport, CT: Praeger, 2006.

Deanna Lyn Wilkinson — *Guns, Violence, and Identity Among African American and Latino Youth.* New York: LFB Scholarly, 2003.

Franklin E. Zimring — *The Great American Crime Decline.* New York: Oxford University Press, 2007.

Periodicals

Bob Adams — "Gun Control Debate," *CQ Researcher,* November 12, 2004.

James D. Besser — "Gun Craziness," *Baltimore Jewish Times,* April 27, 2007.

Steve Chapman — "Should We Have Gun Control for Psychotics?" *Chicago Tribune,* May 3, 2007.

Philip K. Cook
and Jens Ludwig
"Does Gun Prevalence Affect Teen Gun Carrying After All?" *Criminology*, February 2004.

Selwyn Duke
"Assault on the Weapons Ban," *American Thinker*, September 14, 2004.

Rick Hacker
"Guilty—Even When Proven Innocent," *Handguns*, October/November 2006.

Kevin Johnson
"Easy Access to Guns Is Tough to Battle," *USA Today*, June 14, 2007.

Karen Judy
"What to Do About Guns and Violence," *Pediatric News*, July 2007.

Don B. Kates
"The Laws That Misfire," *Recorder*, September 1, 2006.

Don B. Kates and
Gary Mauser
"Would Banning Firearms Reduce Murder and Suicide? A Review of International and Some Domestic Evidence," *Harvard Journal of Law & Public Policy*, Spring 2007.

Tom
Krattenmaker
"A Pious Nation?" *USA Today*, June 11, 2007.

John Lemaire
"The Cost of Firearm Deaths in the United States: Reduced Life Expectancies and Increased Insurance Costs," *Journal of Risk and Insurance*, September 2005.

Robert A. Levy
"A Victory for Self-Defense," *Washington Post*, March 12, 2007.

Michael Luo   "Privacy Laws Slow Efforts to Widen Gun-Buyer Data," *New York Times*, May 2, 2007.

Paul Marks   "The Shocking Use of Police Stun Guns: Do Non-lethal Taser Stun Guns Really Offer Police the Safe Alternative to Firearms That Their Makers Promise?" *New Scientist*, November 12, 2005.

R.D. McGrath   "Making Our Schools Safe: The Virginia Tech Shooting Rampage Highlights the Vulnerability of Our Schools to Gun Violence, but the Answer to the Problem Is Not More Gun-Control Laws," *New American*, May 28, 2007.

John A. Michener   "Crime Scene Liability: When a Crime Occurs on Your Property, Who Is Responsible?" *Risk Management*, May 2005.

Carlisle E. Moody and Thomas B. Marvell   "Guns and Crime," *Southern Economic Journal*, April 2005.

John C. Moorhouse and Brent Wanner   "Does Gun Control Reduce Crime or Does Crime Increase Gun Control?" *Cato Journal*, Winter 2006.

Joan Murphy   "Lethal Weapons," *Baltimore Jewish Times*, March 9, 2007.

Andrew Stephen   "The Unmentionable Causes of Violence," *New Statesman*, April 30, 2007.

Will Sullivan, Chitra Ragavan, and Chris Wilson   "An Uphill Climb for Gun Laws," *U.S. News & World Report*, April 30, 2007.

Chet Williamson   "Murder and the Gun Maker," *Worcester Magazine*, January 18–24, 2007.

Franklin E. Zimring   "Firearms, Violence, and the Potential Impact of Firearms Control," *Journal of Law, Medicine & Ethics*, Spring 2004.

Index